FROM
COASTAL COMMAND
TO CAPTIVITY

FROM
COASTAL COMMAND
TO CAPTIVITY

by

Wing Commander
WILLIAM JAMES HUNTER

with an introduction by his son
DR ALLAN HUNTER

LEO COOPER

First published in Great Britain in 2003 by
LEO COOPER
an imprint of Pen & Sword Books,
47 Church Street,
Barnsley
South Yorkshire,
S70 2AS

ISBN 0 85052 991 3

A catalogue record for this book is
available from the British Library.

Typeset in Sabon by
Phoenix Typesetting, Burley-in-Wharfedale, West Yorkshire.

Printed in England by
CPI UK

Contents

Acknowledgements

Jim Hunter did not write an acknowledgements section before he died, and so if anyone has been missed out I can only apologize, and offer the assurance that the omission is in no way intentional.

The largest debt is, of course, to Elsa Hunter, Jim's widow, who encouraged his writing while he was alive and was generously supportive of this book project throughout. Of those who contributed photographs, information, anecdotes and moral support I would mention above all Jim's sister Mrs. Betty Moorley, and of course Mrs. Iris Simmons. Jim would surely have wanted to acknowledge Roy Conyers Nesbit as well as his friends from the 217 Squadron reunions, who advised and shared ideas as to how he could best shape his narrative. Sadly, the reunions are more sparsely attended with the depredations of each passing year.

Research assistance was generously provided by the Imperial War Museum, The RAF Museum Hendon, and the Air Historical Branch. In the USA I was materially assisted by the generosity and dedication of the staff of Curry College Library. I am also grateful for a grant from the Faculty Welfare Committee and for support from Dean David Fedo, which helped this project to completion. Joan Manchester was a miracle of quiet efficiency in preparing the electronic format. Tom Hartman was the perfect editor in every way, and Henry Wilson's kindness and professionalism was a pleasure and a reassurance at every stage. To Catherine Bennett I owe my gratitude for her critical acumen, understanding, and support. She also produced the excellent maps of the forced marches and corrected and redrew Robert Buckham's diagram of Marlag Nord.

The final acknowledgement must go to the International Red Cross who, as Jim said, "Kept us kriegies alive through those years."

Introduction

In the grey pre-dawn light of 25 July 1941 six Bristol Beaufort Is of 217 Squadron warmed up on the airfield at RAF St. Eval in Cornwall. At 5:30 am, weighed down with bulky landmines that stuck out beyond their bomb doors, they rumbled down the runway one by one and clambered into the sky. The crews scanned the horizon with some anxiety. It promised to be a clear day and they needed cloud cover for what they had ahead of them. They were due to rendezvous with torpedo-carrying Beauforts from 22 Squadron – their orders to find and attack the battleship *Scharnhorst*, surely one of the most dangerous ships on the sea at that time. She was a foe they had faced before. Two nights earlier 217 Squadron Beauforts had bombed her at La Pallice. Now the *Scharnhorst*, escorted by six destroyers, was somewhere in the Bay of Biscay, making a dash for the safety of Brest harbour with its guns and its repair facilities.

The weather quickly worsened, providing the much-wished-for cover from enemy aircraft, but in the cloud and patchy mist the force became separated and only one of the Beauforts was able to find the target. Spotting a large wake in the sea below them, they flew along it, hoping to catch their quarry unawares. In fact the cloud was so thick that it wasn't until they were directly above it that the Beaufort crew saw the huge vessel. There was no time to drop the mine. They had to go round again. It was whilst attempting a second run that the lone Beaufort ran out of cloud cover and immediately encountered a storm of flak. Within seconds the aircraft was hit several times. Moments later it struck the waves as it crash-landed, broke up and began to sink. Sergeant 'Pip' Appleby, the W/Op (Wireless Operator), was killed and the pilot, Squadron Leader Les Collings, was wounded. My father, Pilot Officer Jim Hunter, who was the navigator, and the A/G (Air Gunner), Sergeant Ted Taylor, both suffered minor injuries.

The survivors were picked up by a German ship, and so began their nearly four years in *Kriegsgefangenschaft*, as prisoners of war, or 'kriegies' as they became known.

The small Rowney watercolour book in which Jim recorded his pictures of PoW life, and which are reproduced here, sat on various shelves for over 40 years before he thought of doing anything with it. It travelled with him from prison camp to prison camp, across Germany on the forced marches away from the Russian front, then from one posting to the next throughout his career in the peacetime RAF, and when he retired at age 55 it was installed in his study. There it sat next to his Flying Log Book. Into this he had carefully pasted three small slips of paper. They were the meticulously recorded details of being shot down. He had kept these pages safe from prying German eyes throughout his captivity, just in case he ever had to explain to an RAF Board of Enquiry what had happened to the aircraft. At the top of the page he wrote, "Total time on last 'Op' 3yrs. 09 mths. 15 days 07 hrs. 27 m."

About ten years ago, in response to enquiries from the family, he began to write down his wartime experiences. To these he added many photographs taken at the time, as well as press cuttings and other pieces of memorabilia, and his PoW paintings. Jim chose to organize the material in the form of a direct narrative, almost entirely without what novelists call 'backstory' – the personal details that make up so much of life. He starts it on the day before he was shot down, using the timeline to show an average day in a Coastal Command squadron in wartime, as the airmen come together and prepare for an attack. For him the story was about the events, and what they show, not specifically about him or the minutiae of his world. He often writes about the things he and others did, or shared, and as a result this is much less a memoir of personal impressions than of shared experiences.

While this allows him to impart a huge amount of information in a compressed form it also means that certain things are left unsaid. Some of them are too important to be omitted. My purpose in writing this introduction is to fill in some of the things that were not written, but which he told me or which came from reliable sources. In this way I will attempt to provide a wider context that will help the reader understand some of the references.

The first and most obvious thing that Jim leaves out are details of his family, his background and how he joined the RAF. These matter because they shed light on an unusual aspect of the memoir – that when men enlisted in 1939 and 1940 to serve their country they did so fully aware that this was a class-based society in which certain prejudices still counted. Jim was not of the class from which officers normally came. He was the oldest of the three children of William and Florence Hunter. William had been a horse trainer for the Marquess of Bute but had lost everything when a fire on board ship destroyed his stock of horses. By the time Jim was born, in 1920, William was employed as a mine surface worker at Machen, in Wales. Times were hard and the family lived with Florence's parents for several years. Then they moved to Surrey and in the 1930s managed to get a council house in Coulsdon, near Croydon. At about this time Jim won a scholarship to Caterham School, a public school well beyond the family's means.

One event that stands out from this time is that Jim invited his school friends to a birthday tea (he was probably 13), and his mother worked hard to provide delicious treats. Although his neighbourhood friends arrived promptly and in great good humour, not a single one of his school friends appeared. The boys at Caterham School were, for the most part, from wealthy homes, and in those class-conscious days their parents might not have allowed them into a council estate. If Jim was shy about writing his memoirs it may have been because he had learned early on that others would, and could, judge harshly because of prejudice.

After leaving Caterham he became a bond bearer in the City of London and later he was promoted to be a very junior clerk in

Barclay's bank. For many like him this was to be the first step towards a successful career in banking and he enjoyed the work. But rumours of war were everywhere and Jim felt he would be needed.

When war seemed imminent Jim cycled over to present himself at his local RAF recruiting station. They took his name and address and sent him home. He turned up every Saturday for the next few weeks, just to remind them of his existence, until, one day, they seemed to take him seriously. They gave him a medical examination, measured him for a uniform and told him to await orders. Several weeks later these arrived and he was off to begin training.

As aircrew under training he was the lowest form of life in the RAF, and every long-serving corporal seemed to want to impress that on the new recruits. "They had us saluting them all the time because they knew that we'd very soon be aircrew, and then they'd be saluting us," he said. Discipline at this point seems to have been arbitrary and harsh. Walking across the airfield one day Jim managed unknowingly to break some boundary rule. This earned him a month of extra duties, including scrubbing toilets. Each day's scrubbing made him aware of two things. The first was that his mother had earned the bulk of the family income as a housekeeper for two elderly spinsters, and the second was that he was going to do everything he possibly could to make sure he became an officer.

The camp itself was barren and cheerless. Single-storied buildings of dull red brick with corrugated roofs, or wooden sheds on concrete blocks, seemed to make up the bulk of the freezing cold accommodation. Food in the mess hall was basic. A favourite joke at mealtimes was to sprinkle pepper on one's food, and by the dexterous use of gentle blowing and the howling draft that ran through the place whenever the door opened, one could get most of the pepper to drift on to one's neighbour's plate. We may smile at the schoolboy humour, but it's worth remembering that when people play with food it's usually because it's inedible to begin with. And that was surely the case because around this time Jim volunteered for extra kitchen duty so that he could have better chance of eating properly. He was particularly proud of his custard, made in ten-gallon batches.

He does not mention basic training in his memoir, although he preserved some photographs of his class. He did sufficiently well because he went on to operational training. Originally he put himself down to be a pilot, but in those anxious months of 1940 there were still too few aircraft, and like many others he was asked to choose a second option with the chance of being a pilot when more aircraft became available. He chose to train as an Observer. At that time an Observer's wing was highly prestigious, as the Observer had to be able to navigate, operate the guns, the radio, and arm and aim the bombs. In fact he had to be able to do almost everything. Jim mentions that he spent a number of his off-duty hours in the 'Link' trainer gaining the rudiments of piloting skills, just in case they might be needed.

In the dark days following Dunkirk it seemed there might be little chance to do any of this. At one point Jim's entire class was briefed that in the event of an invasion they were to take off in Tiger Moth biplanes and drop hand grenades on the advancing Germans. Desperate measures indeed, and hardly likely to be effective. In some ways the plan tells us only too clearly about an RAF command structure that was more anxious to be seen to be doing something, no matter how dangerous, than to be doing nothing. Ordinary airmen were expected to pay the price.

These days were not without other dangers. Bombing practice was undertaken by using the obsolete Fairey Battle. The Battle was a large single-engined monoplane that had suffered disastrous losses in France, and had promptly been withdrawn from front-line service. The bravery of the fliers was never in doubt, but the effectiveness of the aircraft was. Although an excellent trainer it wasn't an up-to-date bomber and had inadequate space for a bomb aimer. In order to overcome this difficulty some of these aircraft had been hastily modified by having a hole cut in the underside of the fuselage so that a bombsight could be placed in a position suitable for aiming the 25lb practice bombs slung under the wings. After take-off the trainee had to slide out of the gunner's seat behind the pilot and wriggle down to the bombsight. There, lying on his stomach, squeezed under the glycol coolant tank, unable to see forward adequately, he was expected to perform miracles of accuracy.

The bombsight itself was a Mark IX, a bulky article with various protruding rods on which the vectors were set, the whole thing needing careful adjustment and a perfectly straight and level approach to the target. It cost the equivalent of a junior officer's salary for a year. Since this particular Battle had no intercom at the improvised bombardier's hatch, communication with the pilot was primitive. In order to direct the pilot on to the target the trainee was supplied with a long stick with which he was told to prod the pilot's leg. Two prods meant fly further left, one prod meant right.

While the trainee was aiming and prodding with his stick, the glycol tank had an annoying habit of boiling over its header tank and dropping scalding liquid on his back and neck. This was not too bad if it fell only on the thick Sidcot flying suit. One simply felt pleasantly warm until one had to return to the observer's seat, whereupon the drafts made the liquid very cold indeed and the poor damp individual soon froze.

On one such trip the glycol tank burst and the aircraft was in immediate danger of overheating. Jim scrambled, soaked, back to his seat, while the pilot, a formidable ex-Polish airforce veteran, throttled back and looked for a place to make a forced landing while he still had some power at his command. The bombing range itself was littered with large boulders and so was not suitable for a landing. Worse still, it was at the top of some steep cliffs and was surrounded by sea. Luckily the tide was out and the pilot decided to try a wheels-up landing on a sloping shingle beach. When the plane finally came to a juddering standstill, just short of the cliffs that rose before them, both men exited as fast as they knew how, expecting at any moment that the fuel would explode. They sprinted up the beach and waited for the whoosh and the flames, which did not in fact happen.

They surveyed the scene from a safe distance. How the pilot had managed to keep the aircraft right side up was beyond them to understand. He must have judged the height perfectly and stalled the plane in such a way that it did not dig in and flip end over end. Taking a moment or two to recover their breath, they noticed that the tide was now coming in. Soon their aircraft would be awash.

Back at base, hours later, they reported to the duty officer who took them straight in to the Commanding Officer. Jim was the first to be addressed.

"Hunter, where is your bombsight?"

"In the aircraft, Sir."

"It was signed out to you. You are responsible for that bombsight. It is very valuable."

"I expected the aircraft to burn, Sir. I thought I might be more valuable to the Air Force than the bombsight, Sir."

"Well it didn't burn, did it? So where is the bombsight?"

"The tide was coming in rapidly, Sir. Couldn't reach it."

"Poor show. Loss of valuable Air Ministry equipment. You may be facing a charge." He then turned to the Polish pilot.

"And what do you mean by crashing your aircraft? That's a serious offence. There will be a full investigation."

The Pole looked thoroughly disgusted and growled out his reply through the thickest of Slav accents. "If you court-martial me," he announced in a threatening rumble, "I will desert." He then turned and walked out, leaving the door open.

Jim had no more patience with the Commanding Officer than the Pole had. The difference was that he was still an enlisted man and had to keep quiet, while the Pole was an officer.

No more was said about the incident. In the photographs that Jim preserved is one of his bombing and gunnery class, clad in their Sidcot suits, standing in front of a Battle, two trollies of bombs in the foreground. All fifteen are smiling. Three survived the war.

It was a proud day when Jim received his commission as an officer. From now on he would be on active duty, flying into combat. He would be with highly trained professionals, all of them with a valuable job of work to do, and class prejudices would, he hoped, no longer apply.

His examination results were sufficiently good for him to be posted, in April 1941, to 217 Squadron, which had recently been re-equipped with the new Beaufort bomber and torpedo attack aircraft. The Beaufort was a handsome all-metal aircraft, and Coastal Command were pleased to get it, if only because it was so much more suitable than the docile but ageing Ansons they had been flying up to that point.

Since the sea is a vast featureless landscape over which to fly, and because many sorties were flown at very low level, accurate navigating was essential. Only the best navigators were sent to Coastal Command. Plotting and calculating had to be quick and accurate in an aircraft that was often buffeted by air currents, frequently at night, and usually in bad weather. There was no room for errors. Crossing the blacked-out enemy coast one had to be able to tell instantly from a line of breaking surf where one was, and that is no easy task. In addition, at this time Beauforts were used for mine-laying, and these had to be positioned in the very mouths of enemy harbours, a task of delicacy that required great courage. 217 Squadron contributed greatly to enemy ship-ping losses in this unglamourous way. In flight log books it is referred to as 'gardening'. Most of the squadron had not yet been trained in torpedo attacking roles, and so bombing, mine-laying and anti-submarine work were the main occupations.

Handsome though the Beaufort may have been, it was not very fast and was not well armed. Group Captain Guy Bolland, who commanded 217 immediately before Jim joined the Squadron, considered that daylight raids using Beauforts were all but suicidal and he insisted on night attacks only. Faced with the much faster Me109, the Beaufort's defensive machine guns could put up an estimated 11 ounces of .303 calibre bullets as compared with the Messerschmitt's 12 lbs of cannon and machine gun fire in the same amount of time, with the added threat of explosive cannon shells. It is worth bearing this in mind when we recall that

Bolland was relieved of his command at 217 for his candid views, just before Jim arrived, and that Jim's attack on the *Scharnhorst* was made during daylight hours when fighters could certainly be expected.

Naturally, Bolland's view would not have been made available to the crews at the time for fear of its effect upon morale. In support of this grim outlook we have the following quotation from Bolland's obituary, which appeared in the *Daily Telegraph*, 7 March 2001:

"In March 1941, when the potential menace of *Scharnhorst* and *Gneisenau* to Britain's Atlantic shipping meant that Beauforts had to attack in daylight, Bolland declared all of his squadron's aircraft unserviceable. 'There was no possible chance of any of my aircraft getting anywhere near Brest,' he later explained, 'and even if they did and were lucky enough to hit the ships the damage would have been negligible.' [. . .] Bolland then reported to Plymouth where he told his air marshal and an admiral that 'sending young men to their deaths on useless missions is not on.' The visit cost him his command."

Again, there is a strong sense of the High Command being desperate to be seen doing something with their forces, even if they were appallingly wasteful of human life, for what was sometimes no real return. Jim was well aware of this mood. When he writes of the proposed attacks on the battleship *Bismarck* he notes that the plans were doubly alarming because the crews were explicitly told they would not have sufficient fuel to return to base, even if they were lucky enough to survive the attack itself. Ditching a Beaufort in the Atlantic was hazardous enough, but in those frigid waters exposure would surely have killed anyone who got out alive in a matter of minutes. Fortunately the *Bismarck* was sunk before the mission could become reality.

Was Bolland right in his views? Who can say? The *Bismarck* was sunk because it had its rudder crippled by a Fairey Swordfish torpedo attack that killed almost all the attacking fliers. But that one lucky hit was all that was needed to allow the Royal Navy to get close enough to finish the job. In fact the antiquated Swordfish had an odd advantage: they flew so slowly that the *Bismarck's* guns couldn't lock on to them, as they were all geared for faster aircraft speeds and so the gunners had to resort to guesswork. The result? An Atlantic raider was sunk, which was tactically significant, the Royal Navy's pride HMS *Hood* was avenged and British prestige remained intact. Yet one could argue that the real stranglehold that had to be broken was the U-Boat menace to merchant shipping, which was far more destructive. And Beauforts could be effective against U-Boats.

Bolland's views can also be questioned in the light of a Beaufort attack by 22 Squadron on 6 April 1941, a matter of days after he had been removed from 217. A force was sent to attack the *Scharnhorst* and *Gneisenau* in Brest harbour. Arriving at first light a lone Beaufort flown by Pilot Officer Kenneth Campbell flew towards the *Gneisenau*, releasing its torpedo before it crossed the inner mole which protected the ship. The torpedo flew over the mole and entered the water with just enough room to allow it to settle to the correct depth for its run. It struck the moored *Gneisenau* squarely amidships and nearly sank it. The Germans had not believed it possible to launch a torpedo successfully in such a small space and had not deployed sufficient anti-torpedo netting. Campbell and his crew almost certainly did not live long enough to see the results of their daring. The Germans gave the crew a funeral with full military honours. Even they had been surprised by the courage shown. Campbell received the V.C. posthumously.

No one could doubt that these battleships had to be challenged, and no one would deny that the cost in aircrew lost was horrendous. Yet we must consider the results of all this – that Hitler's battlefleet was never very successful. They spent much of the war scurrying from safe harbour to heavily defended anchorage, desperate to avoid the attentions of the RAF and Royal Navy. In the long run this campaign, so expensive of RAF lives, has to be seen as a victory. The battleships were rendered ineffective because, faced with the determination of RAF attacks under impossible conditions, Hitler's navy was put on the defensive and it ceased to be an effective aggressive force.

In truth, the RAF crews knew their equipment was not of the best. Stories of weaponry and equipment failures were all too prevalent. On at least one occasion Beauforts were armed with bombs of the wrong type for the targets concerned; in this case it was an earlier encounter with the *Scharnhorst*, in June 1940. After pressing home their attack the dismayed crews saw their bombs explode harmlessly on the armoured decks, or bounce off. Whether or not the armour-piercing and semi-armour-piercing bombs that should have been available could have done much more against the thickness of steel plate involved is also in doubt. Roy Nesbit writes in detail about this in his book *Torpedo Airmen* (Kimber, London, 1983).

Jim's aircraft was originally armed with semi-armour-piercing (SAP) bombs for the attack described in this book, but was then re-equipped with a landmine. The SAP bombs could not have caused much damage to the *Scharnhorst* on account of the low height from which they would have to be dropped if there were to be any hope of hitting the target. This type of bomb was only effective if allowed to achieve its terminal velocity and thus have some chance of punching its way through the armour plate. On several occasions 217 Squadron was issued with landmines – codenamed 'magnums' – presumably because of the lack of suitable bombs. A landmine could be highly destructive against buildings and docks because of its lateral blast, but it suffered from two main disadvantages. The first was that it was very hard to aim, since it had no aerodynamic properties at all. It just tumbled. The second was that it had to be slung under the Beaufort with the bomb doors open. This slowed up the aircraft considerably.

Beauforts themselves were demanding aircraft to fly. Pilots had to concentrate every second and often had to use considerable physical force for hours on end to keep the plane flying in trim. The twin-engine design of the early versions was also not entirely satisfactory, and the failure of one engine on take-off or landing was usually fatal for all concerned. In fact the Taurus sleeve valve engine had one great disadvantage as far as Beaufort crews were concerned – there was no capacity for flying very far on one engine. Even with the propeller fully feathered to reduce drag the aircraft would lose altitude. This could be rectified by closing the cooling louvres on the second engine, which is what the Pilot's Notes advised. This further reduced drag but caused the functioning engine to overheat rapidly and so was not much of a solution. Late in 1941 the new and more powerful Wasp engines overcame this problem, but that was too late for many aircrews.

When Jim writes of his pilot's actions after the Beaufort was hit he does not spell out how dangerous any airframe damage was for that type of plane. He describes one engine as out of control and the other as belching smoke. With a more tractable aircraft this would be alarming enough, but with a Beaufort it would be nearly miraculous for the plane not to cartwheel into the sea, killing all aboard. Jim does not explain this to the reader, but to those who know about the Beaufort's more unpleasant foibles I can only say that I am astonished that Les Collings was able to make such a successful crash landing. Hollywood has shown us images of World War Two aircraft suffering terrible damage and still limping home, and that is the stuff legends are made from. The Beaufort was not, by any stretch of the imagination, as stable, as forgiving, or as safe in routine operation. Jim plays down the inadequacies of the Beaufort and refers only briefly to the under-powered Taurus engines.

Even so, the Beaufort was much loved by many of the crews who risked their lives in it. Later in the war it was to be very successful against Axis shipping in the Mediterranean. Patrick Gibbs' *Torpedo Leader on Malta* (recently re-issued by Grub Street Press) describes this campaign fully. It was also manufactured in large quantities in Australia where it served in modified form (designated as the Mark VIII) throughout the Far East until the end of hostilities.

Jim took part in some sixteen attacking sorties of one sort or another. Most of these were mine-laying, with bombing runs on

12

Brest, which was then considered the most heavily defended harbour in the world. He also records in his flying log book going on U-Boat patrols. On 26 June one was sighted and attacked; it dived and the depth charge bursts were seen to be close to the vessel, with an oil slick appearing on the surface.

Two days earlier, while on a patrol, they had spotted three enemy aircraft in the area and, using cloud cover, they manoeuvred for an attack on a lone Ju88. Since the Beaufort I had only one forward-firing machine gun mounted in the wing and a rear facing turret with two machine guns, it was not really a match for a Ju88. Yet they had no doubts. A lively exchange occurred and the Ju88 dived abruptly into cloud, sending back wild streams of tracer, and was not seen again.

It is my feeling that Jim chose not to write about these things in his memoirs because on the one hand he did not want to be seen as bragging, and on the other he did not want it to seem as though he was complaining about the shortcomings of the aircraft and tactics. I think it may have been because he felt this would be disloyal to the RAF, and to his comrades (few of whom survived), and might be seen as making excuses. This was the aircraft they had, and that was that. One did not complain. That would have been too much like asking for pity.

In addition I think he delayed writing for so long because there were by war's end so many people who had done things that had been more glamourous, or spectacular, that it hardly seemed right to him to talk about "his bit". Some of this reticence, I'm sure, had to do with becoming a prisoner of war. I have no doubt that many prisoners of war on both sides survived to lead perfectly happy lives for many years, and yet I cannot help but think that for most there was always likely to be a sense of having been chosen by fate to be outside the main action. Jim makes mention of this towards the end of his memoir.

These days there are many terms we could use to describe this state of mind. Survivor Syndrome, which is the sense of shame at having survived when others haven't, might be one that would apply. Brave men who have shown repeatedly that they *are* brave, may not, in fact, feel they have done as much as they could. For many this can only have been increased by the shock of returning home to a changed landscape – to a neighbourhood that might have been bombed flat; to seek a sweetheart whom one discovered had married someone else; to find friends and relatives who may have been long dead. In all this it's easy to see that many PoWs must have thought no one would really be interested in their experiences. Many stories have doubtless been lost in this way.

With regard specifically to this particular operation against the *Scharnhorst*, there are, for example, some unanswered questions raised by Jim's memoirs which beg to be examined now. The first would be: why did Jim's aircraft attack alone? And we might also ask, why he was the only one to find the *Scharnhorst* that day? There are no surviving records to clarify this but Jim's own comments can be helpful. What happened to the other aircraft? The detachment from 22 Squadron did not even set out, so why were those from 217, who were to be the diversion, allowed to continue? And where did they go?

One answer may be seen in Jim's comment that Sergeant Pip Appleby, the radio operator, had always been a radio enthusiast. He had a habit of dismantling the whole set if he wasn't satisfied with its functioning. Since strict radio silence was the order of the day there was nothing wrong with this. Was there a recall signal which he missed? It's very possible that at this time the Germans were able to mimic the RAF call signs and that they issued a bogus recall signal to the attacking force. The Germans had certainly used this tactic on other occasions. 217 Squadron Station records indicate that the other aircraft returned, and 'duty performed' was written after their serial numbers, which could be consistent with a recall. The ever-zealous Pip Appleby, tinkering with his set, would have been unaware of any such message. And so they flew on through the thick cloud, alone against a battleship.

This detail is important, because the RAF had learned by mid-1941 that the best way to achieve success against enemy shipping was to attack with large quantities of aircraft whenever possible, often including a diversionary assault. This meant the attention of the enemy gunners was distracted by the sheer number of targets attacking from several directions, and the torpedoes that were launched would therefore be difficult to avoid, or 'comb', since they would all be on different tracks.

This method was perfected later in the war when the newer Beaufighter, escorting torpedo-carrying Torbeaus, and often supported by Mosquitos, devastated German convoys in the North Sea. The method was simple: the Beaufighters and Mosquitos would attack the escort vessels and flak ships directly, using rockets and cannons, and 'suppress' the defensive fire. Quite naturally the flakships would fire back against their attackers and choose those targets that threatened them rather than the Torbeaus which were lining up on the cargo vessels. Often the rocket attacks against escort vessels were so fierce and so successful that the flak ships were sunk, leaving the main target all but defenceless against the torpedoes. This was the way it should have been done. In 1941 the resources did not yet exist.

In Jim's case his aircraft was the only one of this strike force to reach the target, and his Beaufort was equipped with a large land-mine, which would quite possibly have been effective against the supporting destroyers. The orders, however, had specified that if the aircraft were separated they were to aim for the battleship itself. So it became necessary to drop this mine (which, as we have noted, had no aerodynamic qualities at all) accurately upon a heavily defended target, knowing that a landmine only had the ability to produce blast. If it had hit the *Scharnhorst* it would have made a big bang and not done much else. If it managed to drop into the sea next to the hull or just in front of the bow there was a chance of doing some damage. The fact that no one else had turned up for the attack was not material. Their orders were to find the target and attack. This they did.

From the moment they had seen the *Scharnhorst's* wake through the broken cloud and mist Jim and his crew knew they were committed to an attack. They also must have known that

15

there would be no point in waiting for other aircraft to turn up, as that would have squandered any slight advantage of surprise. Luckily the cloud cover meant they had some chance of avoiding defensive fire and enemy fighters, at least for the first run in. But they all must have been fully aware that if they could see the *Scharnhorst* clearly enough for a good attack then she would be able to see them. They were pretty sure they wouldn't be coming back from this one.

As it happened, visibility was so poor that they were directly over the battleship before they saw her. There was no chance to release the mine – which would have overshot badly. I suspect a lesser crew might have been tempted to dump the mine and go home. Pilot Les Collings had no doubt that his duty was to go round again.

It was during this second attempt, with the Beaufort lining up for an attacking run, that the cloud melted away entirely, revealing the Beaufort broadside on to its quarry – an easy target. The Germans had surely been fully alerted after the first pass and they could hear with some precision where the Beaufort was. Later in the war pilots would throttle back their engines and glide into the attack, achieving almost total surprise, but this was no longer possible. The element of surprise was long gone and the shooting had just started.

In an aircraft as noisy as the Beaufort the crew could not hear anti-aircraft fire. They might well have been aware of the streams of tracer, and perhaps of the muzzle flashes of the larger guns, as well as of the rocking of the plane from the shockwaves of explosions. They would also have felt the impact of the heavier shells.

Jim records nothing of his own injuries, perhaps out of deference to Pip Appleby's death and the serious wounds suffered by Les Collings. In fact he was concussed by the impact of the crash landing. One eye was knocked askew with the result that for some time it did not point in the same direction as the other eye. It wasn't until he was in captivity that he met another PoW who had been an optician in civilian life. This man taught him the eye exercises that eventually normalized his sight. Perhaps this concussion helps explain his action of dropping the Syko encoding machine over the edge of the sinking Beaufort's nose. We can choose to see it as the action of a responsible and brave flier, or, quite possibly as the mark of a brave man with minor concussion, since the Beaufort was well known to float no better than the average brick.

Fortunately his conscientiousness did not kill him.

The fact that they were picked up by a German ship so quickly is unusual. Even in 1941 ships were not always in the habit of rushing to rescue downed enemy fliers. The *Scharnhorst*, of course, would not have stopped, and neither would her escorts. Their job was to get out of the area as fast as possible. Either Jim was blessed with a compassionate sea captain or the Germans were sufficiently interested in gathering intelligence from their captives to make the extra effort. Were they afraid that three airmen, bobbing around in their Mae-West life jackets, might be seen by other planes and so lead them to the *Scharnhorst*? For whatever reason, it saved their lives.

Many years later Jim discovered that 25 July was St. James's Day, in fact his 'name day'. He always felt that the luck he had experienced that day might have been because 'his' saint had been watching out for him. Being shot down might have felt like bad luck at the time, but if he had continued operational flying with his squadron his chances of survival would have been practically zero.

Jim makes only passing mention of his escape attempts while a PoW. He certainly did dig a tunnel and it did take him to the far side of the wire, but not quite far enough. The plan was to emerge into a field of standing corn, which would have been perfect cover. Instead it came up short, directly under the sentry's path, and he found himself looking at the sharp end of a rifle. Why does he not mention this episode in greater detail? Tunnels often took weeks to dig, and involved a huge investment of effort. I asked him about this. For one thing he said he always felt that it did not really count, as he hadn't "got out of the hole". For another he said the experience of tunnelling had been most unpleasant and he'd occasionally found it claustrophobic in the extreme,

17

especially when the roof began to collapse, as it did with some regularity.

After this attempt he felt he would be better employed using his expertise to forge documents for others. It would be a more valuable way to use his abilities and would ensure him a place on the escape list, waiting his turn to join a suitable scheme. Forging was a particular skill and in extremely short supply. It required a steady hand, expert ability in calligraphy and exceptional eyesight. It also required the ingenuity necessary to improvise anything while possessing almost nothing. Last but not least it demanded vast reserves of patience. Not many people could muster this, let alone under the difficult conditions of PoW life. Moreover, each escaper needed several sets of papers and there was no point in getting out if one didn't have suitable, and convincing, paperwork. Jim's delight in Oliver Philpot's 'home run' is, in some measure, a vindication of his efforts behind the wire, for he had laboured long and hard on those papers, and they had done the trick.

Perhaps it's worth remembering that the forging of German documents was viewed by the Third Reich as a treasonable and criminal activity. Had he been detected the punishment would have been severe. He could, in theory, have been shot.

The determination it takes to remain reasonably cheerful and productive while in captivity for nearly four years, unbowed, bored out of one's mind for much of the time, is of a different order from courage under fire. It takes fortitude, possibly more than we can readily imagine. This is what these memoirs reflect. It emerges if the reader is prepared to notice it. For instance, in his album, amid the depictions of PoW life, are delicate studies of flowers (surely copied from magazines), nostalgic renditions of such places as Gloucester Cathedral and Chipstead golf course, and so on. Each of these is, in its own way, a reaching beyond the grim realities of captivity, a way of keeping one's spirits up. By contrast, in his pictures of the camp I would suggest that Jim was mindful that this might possibly be the only visual documentation of this aspect of the war, and so he set about recording it. On one page he noted, in neat tiny handwriting, the details of the 'foodacco' food cooperative, complete with prices and various bits of kriegie jargon. On another he wrote down the titles of the music played on their block gramophone, all of which is evidence of his desire to document PoW life and get it right.

The pictures themselves rarely have any people in them apart from figures in the distance. As the camps became more and more overcrowded I am sure the idea of seeing beyond the people to try to depict the place was one of his preoccupations. Each picture is not, therefore, about the personalities involved; it's about the place, a record of the experience which we can see vividly through the physical particularities of the buildings and the things they had to live with.

In this Jim benefited from one great piece of luck. By arrangement with the Germans and the Red Cross he was allowed to enrol in the first part of the B.Sc. course in Engineering which was offered on a postal basis. This was not just a distraction from the run of the mill boredom of captivity but something he truly enjoyed. The added bonus was that he was allowed mathematical books and a complete set of trigonometrical drawing instruments. The surviving engineering drawings of the steam engines he designed and constructed are proof of his application to the educational task in hand. But the great advantage was that he could also use these precise instruments for forging documents. Best of all, they were not contraband, and so could not be confiscated. So he worked diligently at his studies and with equal vigour at his forgeries.

Prisoners were allowed some recreational drawing equipment – otherwise these drawings could not have been done – and we have to assume that the Germans expected nefarious use to be made of some of these items. Perhaps that's one reason Jim did some of these paintings. They showed his captors that he had a reason to own the art equipment he had. I think, also, that he was practising his skills in each picture, trying out methods he could use for forgery, experimenting with colours and inks. Some inks were made in the camps – soot and sardine oil

19

produced a good india ink substitute. Each picture was a training ground.

They made other things as well. Jim refers once or twice to the kriegie practice of brewing alcohol. Fermented prunes, given yeast and time, were a good source, but distillation was what was wanted, since the prune juice didn't taste that good and in any case the purer forms of alcohol were easier to conceal. Distillation is a tricky process. If the temperature is too high, or the liquid is left too long, one gets a fair percentage of 'wood' alcohol. This is best used as disinfectant. If swallowed it can have unpleasant side effects. Jim told me of one occasion when he woke up feeling excessively seedy and unable to see out of his left eye. The right eye would only co-operate if he wanted to look down. The upper hemisphere didn't seem to work at all. He decided to give PoW alcohol a miss from that point on. Luckily he was much better the next day, but he kept his promise to himself. This experience remained in his memory and is perhaps part of what lies behind his description of his room-mate Bob Chadwick's reaction to PoW booze – he tried to climb over the wire.

In fact Jim said that some of the best evenings he had in camp were when a bunch of like-minded people would gather and pool their resources to make a 'hellbrew' using odds and ends of chocolate, cocoa, coffee, tea and anything else that looked as though it would create a tasty brew, and they'd have a party on the strength of that. No alcohol didn't mean no fun.

Food on the whole was scarce and erratic. The International Red Cross parcels were the life-savers, but sometimes these would not arrive for weeks on end, and the German rations were sub-starvation. So food, when it appeared, was not consumed right away. Part was always saved. At Lübeck, in Oflag Xc, it was in very short supply. Tea leaves were used three times (or until "the colour ran out"), then placed on newspaper to dry in the sun ("to get some colour back in"), then used a couple more times. Finally they were dried, rolled and smoked.

Prison life was continually filled with random searches and harassments. On one occasion the whole camp was being moved and, upon arrival at Stalag Luft, all were told to strip naked for de-lousing. This, of course, gave the Germans a chance to search through every piece of kit and extract anything considered contraband. So what could the kriegies do to conceal the pick-axe head they had purloined and had so carefully carried? Fortunately there was one kriegie who had a considerable paunch (obviously he hadn't been there long). They tied the small pickaxe head tightly round his waist with string and rolled his flab over it and the string. When the guards walked along the front of the line of naked men the axe was juggled to the back, and when they walked down the back of the line, the axe was wormed to the front. It made it safely into the camp and had a productive underground life for many months.

Towards the latter part of the war sections of PoWs were moved by train from camp to camp, always in cattlewagons – just like the death camp victims. Conditions were primitive – little light or air and inadequate space to lie down, with a metal drum for a toilet. There was also the danger of being bombed and strafed by Allied aircraft. The kriegies quickly found a way to make themselves relatively comfortable. Those who could got hold of heavy nails or the pegs from railroad ties, or any available piece of iron. A rock and a wrapping of rags made a reasonable hammer that wouldn't hurt the hand. The nails were then pounded into the wooden walls of the cattle truck and the kriegies could lift each other up on to the hooks, wearing the Polish greatcoats they'd been issued, and so converting them into hanging sleeping bags. Buttoned in, one could hang from the wall and despite some discomfort around the armpits one could get some rest, dangling like a bat, until it was time for someone else's turn. Some found it agreeable to rest their feet on the floor. Others preferred to be above it all and give floor space to others.

The determined escapers would, of course, be hacking at the thick wooden floors in hopes of being able to make a good-sized hole. This took a lot of effort for the undernourished captives, and on at least one occasion an escapee got out only to slip between the wheels and the tracks and be crushed to death. Jim recalls that on that occasion, with the war obviously close to ending (according to the broadcasts received from the BBC on the illicit camp radio), the death dampened the enthusiasm for escape considerably. It was around this time that, moving past a pine forest, they watched in amazement through the tiny barred window as a V2 rocket lifted off and, trailing smoke in a long curve, headed for England. They had no idea what it was except that it was obviously not friendly. Germany might be losing but that did not mean the danger was over.

Finally, after nearly four years of captivity, Jim knew the war was nearly over when they were marched away from the advancing Russians. The prisoners walked across Germany in long straggling columns and eventually were handed over to the Allies. These marches have been written about many times, and this occasion was no different in its essentials. The PoWs often did, in fact, end up carrying the guards' rifles for them (since the guards were usually those who were too unfit to go to the front lines). The rifles were always returned without the bolts or the firing pins, which had been disposed of. In fact Roger Simmons, who travelled with Jim, remained on friendly terms with one of the guards for years afterwards, and in 1945 began sending food parcels to him in Germany. He kept this up for several years. This was no small thing as England was not exactly the land of plenty at that time.

Eventually the columns arrived at Lüneberg airfield, which was full of bomb craters, with the PoWs still carrying their kit of waterbottles (usually home made from resoldered tins), spare food and clothes. At the derelict airfield they waited until, at last, the promised Lancasters came in to land. There were some over-eager folks who rushed towards the planes before they had stopped rolling, but order was eventually restored; the kriegies were persuaded to leave some of their bulkier items behind and then scrambled aboard. It was hardly a tidy exercise and men sat in the bomb bay or wherever they could. Jim squeezed himself in behind the navigator, well up front, fascinated by this, to him, new aircraft with all its sophisticated instruments. Then the pilot gave a wave to indicate he was going to take off.

Up to this moment Jim had assumed that quite a few of them would be told to get off to prevent overloading the aircraft – that was one reason he'd scrambled so far forward. Those nearest the door would be out first, he reasoned. "When the pilot waved for take-off I thought: what, with this lot on board? We'll never make it!" They did, just, and lifting off he saw, at the other side of the airfield, a Lancaster in flames. Overweight, it had failed to clear the boundary fence. All aboard were killed.

Back in England he was given a medical check and immediately put on a better diet. He weighed about 90 lbs – about average for a returning kriegie at this time, but pitiful for a six footer. Then he was sent home for an emotional reunion with his family. It was only then that he learned of his brother Donald's death at Arnhem in 1944. Homecoming cannot have been easy.

Home leave was very welcome, even with the sad news, but he was still in the RAF and before long he was required to report back for duty, for the PoWs were expected to make the transition back to normal military life. After all, the war against the Japanese was not over. Old habits learned in captivity were hard to break, however, and four years of resisting German orders tended to be reflected in a similar reluctance to accept RAF discipline. Placed in an RAF camp, complete with barbed wire fences and a guard at the gate, many of the men simply carried out their usual escape plans and disappeared off home. It was much easier than avoiding the Germans had been. Jim took a dim view of this. He wanted to get back to flying as soon as possible and thought that desertion would not look too good on his record of service book.

Small infractions were commonplace, and often done in a spirit of fun more than anything else. On one occasion Jim was in a column of former PoWs being marched across the airfield when one of them spotted a mulberry tree in fruit. The whisper went down the ranks rapidly and, with hardly a blink of an eye, the whole column peeled off, in perfect step, in a gently curving left turn. They reached the tree and set about devouring every last berry. The officer in charge shouted and stormed, turned puce, and, in their own good time, the men fell back into ranks and marched on, the ravaged mulberry tree mute testimony to their actions. It was not that they were hungry, Jim explained, it was just that it seemed like such a waste of good fresh fruit.

Jim had many stories like this.

One last anecdote: on boat race day 1945 the crowds gathered along the Thames to watch Oxford and Cambridge battle it out for the first time in five years. Jim decided to drive up to see it in his ageing Austin 7, together with some friends who, in their cars, made up a small convoy. Along the way Jim caught sight of a group of very scruffy Italian and German PoWs hitchhiking. Without a moment's hesitation he stopped the Austin and crammed as many of them in as he could. A few minutes later the ancient tiny car, sagging low on tired springs, with Italians perched on the running boards and hanging from the rear rack, lurched back onto the road to take them all to a day out along the Thames. Jim would never have spoken about that: the story came to light in a conversation after his death. He would have felt it was too self-serving to have mentioned it.

If I choose to write about it here it's to show that this was a man who held no grudges. In later years, when he served at various RAF bases throughout Europe, he had many colleagues in other services, men who had flown against the RAF, sometimes in Luftwaffe uniforms. This did not get in the way of a good working relationship. Some even became close personal friends. After all, Jim had always liked the German people. It was Hitler and company he didn't care for.

When Jim began to write his memoirs he doubted that anyone would ever want to read them. By the time he had finished he knew he had a story that was worth repeating. He knew he had a record of men's bravery, of their comradeship and spirit, and I feel he had also discovered that these things were greater and more powerful than the atrocities of war. He knew he had somehow made sense of the time he had lived through, and found the core of goodness at the heart of it. It's my belief that writing about these events, in all their sorrow, and with their spots of laughter and joy, he was able to achieve a sense of peace about this part of his life. For writing is a way of making sense of our lives – as Jim says at the end – a way of joining the dots to try and see the whole. In this memoir he was able to bring a sense of form and order to what, at the time, must have felt like random events over which he had little or no control. And it is the arbitrariness of the PoW's experience which is surely the most stressful element. When that is added to the random nature of war itself the effects can be disorientating and frightening.

It's easy for us to say, with these events at comfortable arm's length, that the PoWs must have known that they would survive the war. At the time this was far from being a sure thing. German rations were pitiful, and but for the Red Cross many would have starved. Each day in captivity demanded an effort of will, an insistence that one would be treated properly by one's captors. The Senior British Officer arguing the Geneva Convention with the camp Commandant seems like a cliché to us now. But he was not doing this just to make trouble or to insist on preserving some point of dignity. He, and all such officers everywhere, were engaged in walking a delicate line between insisting on their rights – including their rights to break the rules and escape – and yet not antagonizing their captors so greatly as to cause disastrous reprisals. Jim told me on several occasions that Douglas Bader, the famous legless ace, was not always very skilled at this game. The whole camp suffered dire shortages when Red Cross parcels were withheld in punishment, and sometimes no real gain was achieved. The temporary surges in camp morale that Bader inspired by his demands were, it seems, very soon ground down by plain hunger. Some people were actually relieved when Bader was sent to Colditz.

In 1944, of course, the Germans did lose patience. Americans captured at the Battle of the Bulge were machine-gunned, downed airmen were beaten and sometimes killed, and fifty of the seventy-six men recaptured after the Great Escape were shot, as Jim records. Survival, then, was not assured.

*   *   *

25

Jim died on the last day of February 2002, aged 82, after a long fight with cancer. He had remained in the RAF until age 55, loving the work, and retiring as a Wing Commander. He began writing down his experiences in about 1990, and doubtless fifty years had erased some of the memories, but many of them were so sharp, so strong, that no amount of time could erode them.

1

Countdown in Cornwall

The 24th July was for a few a quiet, relaxing day by the sea or roaming the Cornish countryside for those who, despite the war, or in some cases because of it, contrived to take a last fleeting holiday before things really closed in around them. In some cases no doubt it was a matter of spending a few days with their loved ones before they, or their children, were despatched to some safer haven. In any event there were comparatively few people about. The beaches were practically deserted and there was little movement to be seen elsewhere. In earlier years at this time the Cornish coast with its red sandstone and granite rocks and cliffs paddling in the deep blue of the Atlantic would have attracted, not necessarily the wealthy but predominantly the better off, in considerable numbers. July, after all, was the holiday season; children would be home from school and anxious to take Dad on his annual outing to build sandcastles on the sand whilst Mum would remain in charge of everything else. Today, who they were or where they came from was of little consequence to Charles (Jock) McLean and myself as we threaded our way along the cliff tops and along the winding lanes and paths in the afternoon sunshine. Eventually we would reach our billet, the Waterbeach Hotel in Treyarnon Bay. Squadron aircrew were accommodated in the safety of this little cove some three or four miles from RAF St. Eval, which was reached by the narrow and tortuous roads for which this particular county is renowned.

When I first arrived on the Squadron aircrews were accommodated in the Watergate Bay Hotel. This was a rather gaunt, Victorian-looking place built to last forever. It had a kind of arrogant appearance as it looked out across Watergate Bay. Its interior continued that tradition. Even its elderly staff tiptoed around the place for fear of being heard – or seen! The long dark curtaining too bore a decidedly funereal and sombre appearance. It was, without doubt, no place for the young bloods of the day and, fortunately, it was not long before we were able to move out to the Waterbeach. Both hotels had been commandeered by the Air Ministry for the "duration". On larger airfields aircrews were, for the most part, accommodated in the permanent station messes which were part of the airfield complex. There were, naturally, advantages and disadvantages to both systems. For the time being, therefore, we were comfortably housed in quite delightful surroundings; one might almost say we lived in luxury, for the rooms overlooked the sea where the only distracting sounds were those of the seagulls and the occasional beat of the waves on the rocks.

For obvious reasons the considerate government was not really in the business of pampering us, much as we would sometimes consider ourselves worthy of being spoilt a little. On the contrary, a considerable amount of money had already been spent in trying to acquaint us with the rudiments and skills with which to operate aeroplanes. Rather, it was a kind of insurance policy against losing some of their more costly assets by dispersing them away from the airfields which were frequently under attack. Suffice it to say that if one had to fight a war this was no bad spot from which to do it.

The airfield itself was pretty inconspicuous except, perhaps, for St. Eval church on its northern boundary. It had an imposing, square, red-brown stone tower and was still used by the folk who lived in the area. It was Norman in origin and parts of the original stonework could still be found. The only occasions on which I visited this church were, as I recall, to honour those we knew personally who had come to grief as they took off or landed. There was, of course, many a funeral for those who perished in air raids – airmen and airwomen going about their normal duties or taking shelter in the bunkers around the airfield.

Located several miles inland by road, Royal Air Force St. Eval was the home of 217 Squadron and others who were primarily engaged in the war at sea. 217 Squadron was, in fact, the first squadron to be based here when the field was opened in 1939. It was then equipped with Avro Ansons – an aircraft on which I had done much of my early training. Anyone, and there were many, who had ever flown Ansons will rapidly recall its salient points; the one hundred and some winds of the awkwardly placed undercarriage raising and lowering gear, the delicate nature of its fabric skin, the characteristic clatter of its Cheetah engines, its smell (every aircraft had its own peculiar perfume!). Now the squadron operated Bristol Beauforts, a metal aeroplane powered by two Taurus sleeve-valve engines whose power to weight ratio was not very impressive. In fact the aircraft was incapable of maintaining altitude on one engine, certainly not for very long especially with a load of bombs. And the failure of one on take-off was usually disastrous. The Beaufort was a close relative of the Blenheim. It evolved as a Fighter-Bomber or Torpedo-Bomber and, like many squadrons in those days, its duties were many and varied. Ours consisted, in the main, of attacks on shipping of all kinds – flak ships, submarines, merchant shipping – together with attacks on harbours, e.g. Brest, where the pride of the German navy often sought refuge for repair, and minelaying (which sorties were generally known as "gardening"). Gardening trips were as nerve-racking as any, for they were flown at wavetop height at night. Gardening? Why? We were dropping sea mines or 'cucumbers' usually in an area known as 'Jellyfish' in the Goulet de Brest. Add to any other excitement there might be at the time – such as a lack of visibility, sea mist etc., or a burst of fire from a guardian flak-ship from out of the murk – and the adrenalin could flow quite smartly! Anti-submarine sorties would take us out into the

29

Atlantic with depth charges to seek out, and sometimes find, a surfaced submarine. Shipping was usually attacked with 500 pound or, from time to time, 250 pound semi-armour-piercing bombs and machine-gun fire. Airfields, on the other hand, were attacked from a sensible height with 500 or 250 pound general purpose bombs for the greater blast they would provide.

And so it was that Pilot Officers MacLean and Hunter were making their leisurely way back to the Waterbeach Hotel on this summer afternoon. We aimed to be back by three that afternoon in order to get to briefing by four thirty, this time having been set prior to our departure in the morning. The crews who would be flying had yet to be finalized. This was the usual practice, to leave the selection of crews to just before briefing. Our crew had had the day off because we'd been operating the previous night and hadn't landed until five or so that morning. But we quite expected to be on again tonight.

As we approached our billet we encountered several of the residents sitting on the terrace wall, relaxed and at peace with the world. As we drew level Squadron Leader Collings, my skipper, quietly mentioned that we were on tonight. This evoked no surprise nor question, so, after the usual repartee Jock, who was also on the detail but on the reserve crew, and I went to our room to get ready in time to catch the crew bus, which was due at four, to take us up to operations on camp.

Jock and I shared a pleasant room on the first floor with a view out across Treyarnon Bay. It was impossible not to notice the glistening sea in the afternoon sun although I doubt if we consciously looked out as we methodically gathered our clobber together. The standards of furnishing were not exactly opulent but could be said to be adequate and comfortable. The only decorations were of our own making. They consisted of a puffin's skeleton which Jock had found together with a gull's wing. These he had carefully reassembled and mounted on one of the walls. On another were a couple of Heath Robinson prints we'd found at a stationers in town and an illuminated script or two which I'd drawn. Two of these read, as I remember,

The grave's a fine and private place
But none, I think, do there embrace.

Oh would I were where I would be
There would I be where I am not
For where I am I would not be
And where I would I cannot.

All very erudite but I'm not sure why! Just a couple of thoughts which came to mind – and we put them on the wall.

On the shared writing desk Jock kept one or two of his family snapshots. One was of his sister Effie who I believe lived with their parents in Linlithgow. There was also a picture of another, a very pretty girl whose name I don't recall, Jock's girlfriend. Photographs were not too common in our family. But I did have one which I'd mounted in a wee frame, of a girl I'd known from schooldays but with whom I'd practically lost touch in the last year or so. In fact I could not really claim she was my girl, at least not any more, not exclusively. Her name was Renie. At one time I had placed her inside my small dictionary which I used when writing letters etc. Maybe my spelling didn't improve too much but it was nice to look her up from time to time!

Although with the aid of these few accoutrements we thought the place looked fairly decorative it was nothing compared with Tommy Kerr's room or, for that matter, Graham and Stockley's. Tommy Kerr was a largish Canadian who, during his time at University, had acquired a number of trophies and banners. The inseparable Graham and Stockley, pilot and navigator respectively, were a couple of extroverts who favoured pictures of girls and aeroplanes (in that order). They were an hilarious pair, fairly recently arrived on the squadron who always flew together. They flew very successfully and very courageously and were both awarded DFCs. I think it was for their lone attack on an armed merchantman which they either severely damaged or sank. They and their crew were subsequently killed, as were Tommy Kerr and his crew. As a matter of fact Tommy was shot down before me; I

31

remember on our way out to the aircraft in the crew bus how we joked about our worldly wealth and who we should leave it to. Tommy left me his red MG. I don't know what I had to leave anyone except a silver cigarette case. I do know, however, that I didn't survive long enough to take delivery of Tommy's car.

Just a word about my room-mate Charles MacLean: we were both Observers. We were also trained to perform the duties of other members of the crew, with the exception of the pilot; even then we had both spent a fair amount of our spare time in the Link trainer in order to acquire the rudiments of flying. As we used to say, one never knew. Our primary task was, of course, navigation, with the addition of bomb aiming and gunnery. To these we had added a further, partial skill, namely the management of the radio. We would never claim to be wireless ops, but since we had to rely on bearings taken by radio as a nav-aid we thought it prudent to know how they came about and what their limitations were. Before the war I had been an enthusiastic amateur radio constructor and, I suppose, some of that enthusiasm remained. Another thing which appealed to Jock and me was astro-navigation. This hadn't really formed part of our early curriculum although it had been hinted at as a useful aid. We, therefore, spent a little time working with a method which employed Driesenstock's tables, an American system. Unfortunately sextants were at a premium and, in any case, such equipment would have been virtually useless to us as we flew at low, bumpy levels on most of our ops. Neither was the Beaufort equipped with an astrodome through which to take any star sights. Any shots we might have taken would have been so inaccurate as to be virtually useless. Furthermore, in order to take a successful star shot it was necessary to fly a straight and undeviating course for two minutes at least. No matter how skilled the pilot such refinement was usually out of the question and George, the automatic pilot, was not the kind of experimentation pilots liked to engage in when flying fairly low down. George was not a very reliable chap at all; the kind of thing he would do when he was engaged was to tilt the starboard wing and put the nose

32

down! So although we broadened our navigational horizons this particular aspect, astro-navigation, was of little practical use to us. These activities served to cement our friendship for we both thought we'd one day become ace navigators although our training had been along different channels geographically. No matter, we were both 21. We'd both left school with Matric, high hopes and the optimism of youth – and little else. Jock was 100% Scot but I too could claim Scottish parentage, on my father's side. In addition we shared the same sense of humour or thereabouts.

Now it was time to attend to the matter in hand – preparation for briefing and tonight's op. After a quick tooth clean and a change into uniform we began to collect up the miscellania necessary for flying. Part of this system would be to ensure that we were leaving behind any personal papers, letters or anything which would disclose anything other than our identity should we have the misfortune to land in enemy territory. The barest essentials were catered for by the 'dog tags' we wore around our necks and gave our name, rank, service number and religion. It was also a good idea to throw in a razor and towel in case we were diverted or, as some wags would say, 'Just in case we should land in someone's harem'. Upon reflection I suppose there could be such things in France or Germany. It would all depend upon the quality of the welcome! Diversions were the most likely reason for such precautions, for the Cornish coast in the summer months was very prone to unannounced sea mists. They would simply roll gently in from the sea on an otherwise fine day and obliterate all in their tracks. Whenever this happened there would be no point in hanging around waiting for it to clear. The chances were that fuel would be short after a trip and so it was prudent to make for an airfield which was open. Our usual and nearest diversion was Chivenor in north Devon. I'd done my operational training there during the very cold winter of 1940-41, as I recall.

Well, here we were booted and spurred, so to speak, and I was just wondering if there would be a cup of tea in the offing when Bert arrived with his firm and insistent knock on the door.

"Thought you might like a cuppa tea before you went," he'd say. What timing!

Bert was in his fifties, I suppose. A stocky, greying individual with a slight limp, he was always cheerful, sometimes rather more cheerful than the situation demanded. And, as batmen go, he was not a bad batman either. Well, he kept the room clean and tidy without much reminding from us who were not the tidiest of people, and he'd put one hell of a shine on a pair of shoes. But he could be infuriating at times if we happened to be in the room as he went about his business. He had a tendency to natter constantly. Oh yes, one could tell him to shut up, usually politely, but any silence was generally short lived. He had views on almost any subject. But his favourite, not unnaturally, was the last war. That was, we understood, where he acquired his limp. "It was Wipers," he'd say. "It was different in them days." To us, although we accorded him some respect on account of this, it was all a very long time ago and far away, just as our little job will be one day, I expect. However, a cup of the thick brown solution at this time put a much better complexion on things. And we both thought Bert an excellent batman.

The "chop rate" on the Squadron had been reasonable, I suppose. Since we usually operated singly or in pairs and only occasionally in flights of six or more there were not many occasions when our losses appeared at all serious. It was simply a matter of a crew not returning – very saddening for their friends on the Squadron, but of no earth shattering importance to the unit as a whole. Even so it seemed to be the custom to leave a farewell note and we were no exception. The last thing we did before leaving our room was to place these notes on the desk or the table where they could easily be found and, with any luck at all, they would be sent on if need be by the Committee of Adjustment whose job it would be to look after such matters. I left two notes, one to my parents and the other to Renie even though, as I've said, I hadn't seen her for quite some time. When I first joined the R.A.F.V.R. I had a strong desire to go across to her house – she lived only on the other side of the valley – but somehow I never did. After all, it would have appeared very brash and boastful to have appeared in my new uniform of ACHGD – Aircraft Hand General Duties with the rank of Leading Aircraftsman. (And you can't start much lower than that!) But I also had a white flash in my cap to show that I was aircrew under training! Much later on I did muster sufficient courage to cycle across to her house on what was to be, as it happened, my last leave. But that didn't work out either, for just before I got to her house she had left to return to Stroud in Gloucestershire. Before the war she worked at the Air Ministry in London but had since been evacuated to the country. Such were the thoughts, revived by the placing of my pathetic little notes which I'd written some months ago, as I made my way down the steps to the crew bus waiting in the drive. I quietly resolved to drop her a line when I got back; yes, I'd write to her tomorrow. But just in case there was my note. It was all a kind of superstition really, based on the principal that if one is ready for something to happen the chances are that it won't.

No more day-dreaming. The crew bus was waiting in the front drive, almost impatiently it seemed from the noise of its engine and the blue smoke it exuded.

We weren't the last to arrive so we got a seat – although that was a mixed blessing as the bus negotiated the tortuous and bumpy road to camp. As the last chap leapt aboard we thumped on the roof to let the driver know we were ready and away we went. It was then that I really felt the benefit of the afternoon in the sun and the salt sea breeze as we bumbled in every direction through the beautiful Cornish countryside. I was a delicate soul, probably associated with my fair skin and ginger hair. Whatever it was, I caught the sun with the greatest of ease. And I felt sore! These same characteristics must have earned me the nickname of "Red" or, as the Australians preferred, "Blue". But what's in a name when you've got a sore back!

I remember my first experience of these tortuous roads, months back. Sergeants Appleby and Taylor and myself had been at O.C.U. (Operational Conversion Unit) at Chivenor, near Barnstaple before being posted to 217 Squadron at St. Eval. They were a well matched pair, compatible, quietly efficient and always cheerful. At first we were all SNCOs at Chivenor when we first crewed-up and we all lived in the same huts. Shortly after our arrival, however, I was commissioned and then moved across to the Officers' Mess. Such an event might have had a greater impact in the other services but among aircrew any differences were mainly in our relationships on the ground. Over familiarity between officers and NCO aircrew was certainly frowned upon by the regulars and we of the Volunteer Reserve were left in no doubt of this requirement. In fact it all worked out very well. It was simply a matter of common sense. We were, after all, trying to achieve the same objective, facing the same odds with the result that the "crew spirit" pervaded, and even surpassed all other feelings. It can fairly be said that we were a pretty cheerful crew. Our pilot was Squadron Leader Les "Digger" Collings, RAAF. Digger had previously flown Hudsons, and had already been at St. Eval for some time before we arrived from OCU where we had been crewed-up. Sergeant Pip Appleby and Sergeant Ted Taylor were both Wireless Operator Air Gunners (W/Op AGs) and I was Observer (the then title for navigator and bomb aimer).

Originally our first intended skipper had been posted to another squadron to join a crew there. Then our next skipper-to-be, having completed one tour, was taken off flying for medical reasons. We were beginning to wonder what effect we were having on likely pilots when off we went to St. Eval by train.

Padstow was the nearest railway station and it was there that we took leave of the train and headed for the closest phone box to get some transport to collect us and to tell St. Eval that their troubles were over – we had arrived! As it happened their troubles were not over by a long chalk. They were just beginning, for that night anyway. They were in the middle of an air raid. So we were ordered to find some sort of accommodation, let the base know where we could be found and we would be collected when the opportunity presented itself. Not unnaturally we headed for the nearest pub where we felt we'd be all right till closing time when we hoped something would turn up. Strictly speaking, it was not really a matter of finding a room but just somewhere to put our gear and our heads for as long as it took Jerry to stop disturbing the peace up at camp. As it happened we were made very welcome and even offered a meal. Rationing or no rationing, mine host's wife produced some excellent sausage, egg and fried bread after which we were invited to use the front parlour until the transport could collect us. We had indeed struck it lucky, which, we learned a little later, was due in no small part to the fact that the landlord's son was currently enjoying the rigours of training at Blackpool, also for aircrew. It was not till first light next morning that the transport sought us out and hurtled us, post haste, to the airfield.

That was months ago. Today was different.

The Ops block was neatly tucked away behind tall grassed banks, and it was outside a concrete-lined trough through this protective bank that this load of bodies was disgorged from the bus, eager to learn what this particular night had in store for them. Clutching our various accoutrements we wound our way down the corridor to the main door. There a sentry slapped his rifle butt in salute as we arrived. I used to think that particular duty must have been quite tedious and almost superfluous – for anyone other than the genuine type would surely have been conspicuous. But that was not my particular province or sphere of influence and so he did his two hours on and four hours off in accordance with the rule book. How much more fortunate were we whose duties were completely absorbing. To any casual bystander or even to our friendly guard we might have appeared to be a pretty cheerful lot as we shambled with our kit into the holy of holies. But the chatter diminished as we picked our way cautiously across the highly polished linoleum of the ops room floor. We sometimes imagined floor polishing must have been some kind of occupational therapy for the Ops room staff!

There were six crews plus one in reserve at this briefing, which, by our standards, was slightly unusual. We were pretty sure it would be one of our "regular" targets, the *Scharnhorst* or another pocket battleship, the *Gneisenau*. In a very short time this became quite clear, for the Intelligence officer, Flight Lieutenant Shackleton, had made a number of amendments to his wall charts since we had studied them two nights ago. With our kit parked on a chair we looked and made our own assessment of the situation before the briefing began. It was quite apparent that the *Scharnhorst* was on the move. She was shown approaching Brest from the Bay where we knew she had been because it was at La Pallice that we'd been the other night. We also quickly deduced our attack hadn't been quite the devastating success we had hoped. Digger then joined us, exchanged the usual pleasantries and then remarked, "I thought Bomber Command claimed they'd hit the bloody thing?" For Bomber Command had also taken part in our attack on La Pallice.

I've already explained how we failed to crew up with two possible pilots at OCU, and when we joined the squadron we were a little surprised when we were allocated to the flight commander or the senior pilot on the squadron. More by luck than judgment I'd done pretty well at Nav. school. I remember that my last airborne exercise on which my final assessment was made was with the Chief Instructor. The day was particularly miserable, wet, blustery and with very low cloud. The C.I. was an ex-Merchant Navy officer and although he may well have been very much at home in the raging tempests of the sea he had no head or liking for turbulence in the air, and it was certainly a very turbulent trip that day. In brief he became quite ill in the air but insisted that I complete the trip. I must have done this fairly satisfactorily since we got back to base at the expected time! Although in all fairness I should add that the staff pilots were pretty experienced folk. For instance, Sergeant Hood had already some 2000 hours to his credit and Flight Lieutenant MacIntosh had considerably more as an ex-Imperial Airways pilot. They knew their way around the skies. So although I got 100% for the exercise, which may have contributed in some measure to our situation, it was not really all my fault.

Digger was not the type one would normally have taken as an Australian, at least not according to our preconceived ideas of

Australians to date. I, however, hadn't yet met many. First, he was quietly spoken, well most times, and his accent was more in keeping with that of a southern Englishman. Second, he wore a trim moustache of which I am sure he was justly proud. When deep in thought he would frequently twirl the ends, and when he smiled I thought he bore a strong resemblance to Velasquez's "Laughing Cavalier". When he was vexed, however, that moustache could definitely bristle to the accompaniment of the choicest Australian adjectives. On this occasion he simply gave the starboard end a quick tweak and lit a cigarette.

We had already checked the crew lists to see if any changes had been made; as expected, Jock McLean was in the spare crew and, in the event, they were not required to fly this op. They, nevertheless, attended briefing as normal so that should one of the detailed aircraft go unserviceable the reserve aircraft could quickly fill the breach. There were occasions when the powers-that-be would decide to change one body for another as, for instance, should some member go sick or, occasionally, to insert an experienced member in an otherwise inexperienced crew. I always considered being 'first reserve' a totally unenviable position: there would be the usual build-up to the op and the making of detailed preparations and sometimes it would not be till the last moment that the decision was made. Then would follow the joy of not having to go, although even that would be tinged with a feeling of being left out. If one went, on the other hand, there was the challenge of having to fit into a routine perhaps different from that with one's own crew. Our crew was intact and on this occasion it was Ted's turn to occupy the turret and Pip's to do the WOp-ing. They were both trained to occupy either position and they would take it in turn.

We had not long to wait for the arrival of the Squadron Commander, Wing Commander Leslie "Dickie" Bower. Meanwhile the conversation between Digger and the rest of us was not exactly stimulating; I told him Jock and I had walked back along the cliffs and he mentioned he'd had lunch with Joan, his girlfriend. With very little preamble the briefing was begun.

The situation was given in outline, including last night's op. In short the target was the *Scharnhorst*, one of the German pocket battleships, which posed a severe threat to our shipping, etc., etc. Most of this we already knew from previous briefings when we were, for instance, attacking the docks at Brest. The vital statistics of this battleship were a permanent feature on the briefing notices board. The *Scharnhorst* was launched at Wilhelmshaven in 1936, she had a standard displacement of 26,000 tons and a full load displacement of 32,000 tons. From stem to stern she was 741 feet and carried some 12,500 tons of armour protection. Her armament was as formidable, consisting of nine 11-inch, twelve 5.9-inch, fourteen 4.1-inch and sixteen 1.45-inch guns. In addition she carried two catapult aircraft, He 115s. On this occasion she was believed to be accompanied by six destroyers and the whole lot would be making its way to Brest on the morning of 25 July. In addition to the vessel's anticipated heading, course and speed and its position as accurately as could be ascertained at that stage it was emphasized that we should confine ourselves to attacking the destroyers. The only exception would be in the case of the torpedo squadron not making the rendezvous. In that case we should attack the main target. Such was the briefing being given by the C.O. and the Intelligence Officer, Flight Lieutenant Shackleton.

The briefing continued with few superfluous words, just facts. The main attack was to be carried out by 22 Squadron who would go in first with torpedoes against the main target whilst we were required to act as a diversion by attacking the destroyers which would be escorting her. The torpedo boys would go in at wave-top height. We, on the other hand, would fly at a "comfortable" height of 5,000 feet for bombing. In the event of our being separated from one another, or, in the worst situation, should we not meet the torpedo chaps, we should attack the main target. It was imperative, however, that we should not get involved with those lower down. We had done some torpedo practice runs whilst at OCU but we had never, so far at least, been required to put that training into effect. Whilst it had been fun to practice at low level

40

along Braunton Sands, it was quite another matter to fly an unwavering course towards a target who would pour all the metal it could find at its attacker, and then, having dropped the "fish", to get the hell out of it. On balance we were sure we had the better bargain.

Although we were briefed to fly at 2,000 feet on the way out we knew there would be variations on that theme. For instance it would be necessary to maintain contact with the sea if we were to see what was on it. Furthermore, the aneroid altimeters with which we were equipped, even allowing for several correcting factors which had to be applied, were not accurate to within a couple of hundred feet or so. So, rather than descend blind through cloud, we would maintain contact with the surface visually. Even so we would still have to climb to a suitable height to bomb effectively, for semi-armour-piercing bombs would hardly have reached their terminal velocity below 5,000 feet.

Following previous attacks during the time she had been at Brest and later at La Pallice, the *Scharnhorst* had suffered damage from mines and bombs, which when added to other serviceability problems, had kept her pretty well immobile for several months. None of these was serious enough on this occasion to prevent her undergoing sea trials in the last few days. She did in fact leave Brest, where she had been docked, earlier in the month, since when she had undertaken sea trials and practice firing in the La Pallice roads in the Bay of Biscay on the 23rd. Apparently these trials had promised well and, so Intelligence told us, she had attained a speed of 30 knots and her guns and turrets had performed as planned. We were also told that some minor snags required attention and it was for that purpose she had returned to her anchorage at La Pallice that evening. The RAF had been kept remarkably well informed of this target's progress so that we were able to take advantage of her inability to sail that night. We had been part of that attack, and although we claimed no personal success, it was said that there were five hits scored. With the amount of armour that the ship carried it was hardly surprising that so little damage had been done with our GP or

41

semi-armour-piercing bombs. Consequently, on the evening of the 24th she began her daring run to Brest, albeit at a reduced speed; she was now believed to be capable of little more than 20 knots. The Germans, not least Captain Kurt Hoffmann, her commander, were well aware the defences at La Pallice anchorage were inferior to those at Brest, so the incentive to raise sufficient steam for long enough to make the journey was great. It was during this journey we were to make our attack.

For reasons best known to themselves the Air Ministry had given the *Scharnhorst* and her sister ship the *Gneisenau* the code-names "Salmon" and "Gluckstein" respectively, the names by which we always referred to them. Momentarily my mind sub-consciously flashed back to those now distant days, of 1937/8, when I had been a very junior clerk in a firm of stockbrokers in the City. (Later, however, I graduated to become a very junior bank clerk!) During my stockbroking days my early duties required that I should deliver bearer bonds and stock certificates to brokers and companies within the square mile as fast as my legs would carry me. On these considerable travels I moved for a while in unchartered waters; I had yet to find my way around the City of London. As a reference point I used a corner of Copthorne Avenue in which the most conspicuous shop was a large tobac-conist called "Salmon and Gluckstein". The name fascinated me at the time and because it was emblazoned in gold lettering behind a large glass panel above the window it was easily remembered! It took no more than a fleeting second to recall this rather absurd piece of information, which could hardly have been of any sig-nificance so far as the present situation was concerned.

The briefing concluded with each trade seeing his specialist officer for any final details. On the navigation side it was decided that our best chance of finding the target using such information as we had of last known position, estimated heading and speed would be to employ a plotting technique known as a radius of action to a moving base or, alternatively, a straightforward inter-ception. Neither method was uncommon so I chose the latter as I considered it would be easier to modify should the situation require it. The flight plan could be drawn up in the comfort and tranquillity of the ops room with its adequate lighting and a steady desk! It was imperative to draw up a comprehensive flight plan since it formed the basis of the whole flight; should all else fail this plan could take one to and bring one home again – in theory. When once completed it would be easy to follow, especially in its new, pristine condition. The weather and unplanned manoeuvres, however, played a large part in the chart's final appearance. For instance, at night we could use only the minimum of light when once airborne; a bumpy ride and the encroachment of the inevitable raindrops onto the nav. table really put paid to any pretence at neatness of chart or log. It was not so much a matter of producing a pretty chart as being able to use the information we'd been able to put on it.

Final briefing would take place an hour and a half before take-off, which was planned for 5.30 next morning. Then we'd get the latest intelligence information, an update on the met situation and last minute changes in tactics. We'd also collect the Syko machine with which to decode and encode messages, the colours-of-the-day cartridges and escape money with which to make our way home should we be unfortunate enough to land on the wrong side of the fence! And, of course, the flying rations consisting of a bag of sweets or perhaps a bar of chocolate.

The day was yet young. Accordingly, following the main briefing, it was necessary to go out to our aircraft to check that everything was in apple-pie order – or as near as one could judge at this juncture. We had been allocated "X" which had been delivered only a couple of days back and which we'd been expecting to test fly. Someone else had already done that and the compass, which would, of necessity, have to be swung, had been done by Jock and his merry men about the same time. So I knew I could rely upon the accuracy of the compass cards no matter how much deviation was recorded on them. The armourers were busy loading semi-armour-piercing bombs into the bomb bay and the other tradesmen, fitters, mechs and the radio chaps, were going about their duties of loading ammunition, fuelling, etc. We were not in the position of having a ground crew allotted to a specified aircraft. Nevertheless, we'd got to know a number of them quite well. They were a great bunch with a sturdy sense of humour who didn't take umbrage at being questioned about some aspect or other of what they were doing. They knew jolly well we depended upon them even though they probably didn't give aircrew much credit for the technicalities of what they were up to. Everyone was busy just now, so there was little time for chat. It was after an operation that rapport was at its best. The functioning of the engines was everyone's first concern and they knew as well as we that the Taurus could be temperamental, but if handled with respect would perform well. Engine failure on take-off with a full load could be, and sometimes was, fatal and a dead "donk" in flight meant an early appointment with land or water. When everyone was satisfied he'd done all that was required it was simply a matter of waiting for the crew bus to take us to our respective messes.

It was a fine summer evening and St. Eval was a pleasant, rural sort of airfield with extensive views across farmland and hedgerows. From ground level one could not actually see the sea but anyone with a keen nose could smell it. The coast at its nearest point was only a mile or so away as the crow (or Beaufort) flew. Altogether it was good to be alive; there were few sounds except for the rumble of a vehicle here or there, the twitter of the birds and the inevitable squeal of the seagulls. The absence of any aircraft noise added a touch of drama to the situation, a feeling of something about to happen.

The crew bus came leisurely round the peri-track, picked up a couple of crews as it approached and then stopped for us. We leaped aboard, ready to be graunched and bounced back to the mess. There we'd park our gear in the rooms allotted to us for the night, tidy ourselves up a bit and then make our way to the dining room for a night-flying supper. We'd be assured of the usual bacon, eggs and tomatoes, followed by coffee which we'd take with us to the anteroom where we could read the papers, have a game of snooker or, if one was so inclined, play a hand of bridge.

44

All very leisurely; in fact had one been on holiday I'm sure today would rate as one of the better days – swimming, a pleasant walk along the seashore, an industrious afternoon fussing around the aeroplane, good food and a comfortable bed for the night. All this and being paid into the bargain, and at 14/6d (72½p) a day as a Pilot Officer was, in my view, not at all bad.

As the sun lowered in the sky and dipped into the sea my thoughts turned to an occasion when we'd spent several tense hours on stand-by. The occasion was the expected return of the *Bismarck* to Brest, which was, as I recall, Whit Sunday 1941. The powers-that-be had worked out a wonderful plan to enable us to intercept this ship at sea. The idea was to locate her by means of a normal Radius of Action and then, since she would most likely be beyond our range, we must expect to ditch as we ran out of fuel on our return. To obviate any difficulty, however, there would be high speed launches at the ready. Fortunately for us the Royal Navy had taken up the challenge and, with the courage and skill of the people flying Fairey Swordfish, they had dealt with the *Bismarck* in a most spectacular way. Funny how one recalls the humour of events at the most unusual and unexpected times. At the briefing that Sunday morning, for instance, I recall a couple of WOp/AGs who, when the subject of ditching was being discussed, observed, "When we're in the dinghy how's the Nav going to get a QDM? " (A QDM is the magnetic course to steer to reach a certain point, a course of action sometimes frowned upon by the purist.) Then there was another chap who wanted to know "Approximately how deep it would be at the point of ditching"!

It seems that whilst my thoughts had wandered to useless things I'd quietly come to the end of the magazine I'd been reading. And so to bed.

Morning came round very quickly. Well, it was hardly morning and it seemed an unreasonable time for anyone to do anything but sleep. But at three thirty precisely I found myself scalding the inside of my mouth with what the mess batman called tea. Bert's was a whole lot better than this; furthermore, Bert's had sugar!

The morning toilet was a cursory affair. A quick shave and tooth-clean and that was it and since I was accustomed to setting out my clothes at night for the following morning it took me little time to dress. A quick scan to make sure I had collected everything I'd brought with me and I was on my way to breakfast even though it was not long since I'd last eaten. Nevertheless, I felt in need of a little more sustenance which I washed down with a better cup of tea than the first one that morning. I still hadn't really acquired a taste for coffee. That was to come later – ersatz though it would be.

As ever, the crew buses were champing at the bit, oozing blue exhaust smoke outside the mess, ready to take Pilots and Observers to Ops. The W/Ops and AGs would be taken straight to the aircraft from their mess. The first thing we learned was that the weather on the whole would be good; we might encounter a small front and the winds would be light. The most significant alteration to the plan was the change of bomb load. Instead of SAPs we'd seen being loaded yesterday evening we would now be carrying land mines (magnums). This meant several things. First, our attack would now be from no more than 1,000 feet. Accurate aiming of a landmine with the Mk IX bomb-sight was not really a practical proposition. To offset that, however, it would make a much bigger bang than the 250 lb SAPs. It still had the ballistics of a paving stone no matter how one looked at it. Another snag was the fact that they were too large to fit properly into the bomb bay of a Beaufort so the bomb doors had to be left slightly ajar with the consequent increase in drag and reduction in airspeed. Our previously prepared flight plans would, therefore, need some revision. We'd have time to begin these re-calculations in the ops room and they could be completed in the aircraft, otherwise no problems. That done, we'd muster our gear once more and off we'd set. Negotiating the swing doors with all the clutter we had was always an effort but just as I was preparing to lean my weight against the door the LACW who worked in ops helping with Intelligence, typing, etc., held the door back for me. I made a quick recovery before

46

falling and said hello. She was a nice looking girl with a fresh complexion and auburn hair, very much like Renie as I remember her. I thanked her to which she replied, "Have a good trip – and do come back safely." Now that was a nice thought which added a magic touch to the morning. I probably smiled and blushed and then went on my way rejoicing.

The W/Op and Gunner were already aboard and sorting themselves out; Pip was assembling his box of tricks in the W/Op's compartment and Ted was busying himself polishing the perspex in his turret, for, as he would say, "If you can't see 'em you can't hit 'em." The skipper and I did the usual tour around the outside of the aircraft and I made a point of inspecting the bomb bay primarily to check that the arming pins, so far as one could see with a landmine, were in place in the fuses. A mine carried three in the nose and three more in the tail. Technically, nothing happens to a mine until the arming pins are withdrawn and the fuse is free to operate by dint of the wind turning the little propeller to allow a striker to explode the detonator on impact. Whilst they're in place it's quite safe, although I do remember an occasion when we were diverted to Chivenor and one crew, Sergeants Holliday, Whadcoat and their WOp/AGs had a hung-up mine aboard. The next day we set out for base and we were in the lead. The weather was fine and the flight was no more than thirty minutes. Some five or six minutes into the flight the aircraft behind us just blew up and, so far as I know, the reason for that was never determined. It was assumed that their mine had exploded but it is difficult to imagine a crew taking off without ensuring the pins were intact.

Digger went first up the ladder into the aircraft – there was scarcely room to pass in the fuselage until he had scrambled into the cockpit. I could then crawl into my glasshouse in the nose. It would have been a whole lot easier to have climbed in through the nose had we not been armed with what was known as a 'scaregun', a Browning mounted on the floor and pointing backwards. This could be quite a useful piece of kit in an encounter with another aircraft on any other occasion. Today, however, it would be of no use at all, at least on the outward leg; its angle of deflection was only slight and the chances were that the first shot (and the last!) would hit the projecting landmine! On the other hand it could well come in handy on the return flight should we encounter any nasties.

As the pilot checked around his cockpit I began installing my odds and ends in the nav compartment. The first task was to get rid of the most bulky stuff – my parachute, which occupied a slot on the starboard behind the seat – then to arrange everything around me in its accustomed place. It required a little discipline because without it there was always the risk of some item finding its way to the floor and from there to disappear for ever down the cartridge case chute into the sea and beyond! Having done what was necessary I'd poke my head round to the cockpit to see how Digger was doing. Most things seemed to be where they should be so far as he was concerned and he was just placing his "crib sheet" of headings, times and distances, which I'd prepared for him to enable him to keep track on our progress, above the coaming above the instrument panel. Last came his packet of cigarettes. We were in good time, with several minutes in hand before start up. This was just as well since we should be the first to go.

The grey light of dawn had now given way to a yellowish sky – the portents of a fine day to follow. I'm sure we all hoped there would be just a little cloud in the target area, say 5/8th at around 3,000 feet. That would do nicely. Based upon yesterday's bomb load we would have raised that by a couple of thousand feet!

2

Outward Bound

All was very quiet until the skipper's voice over the intercom announced, " Time to go – final check," to which we reported in turn and waited. The ground crew who had been in position for some time beside the chocks waited for the skipper's signal to start up. The port engine started nicely with the usual cloud of exhaust smoke and purple flames from the rich mixture lapping over the wing's leading edge. The engine was set at fast idle while the same procedure was used for the starboard engine. This was a shade more reticent and required a little more encouragement, but soon it too fired with a slightly better display of purple flame. The propeller gathered speed to keep time with the other until the temperatures and pressures for both engines reached the normal. Then the engines would be run up, the pitch operation of the propeller actuated and the magnetos checked for serviceability. Then back to fast idle once more to await the "green" from the caravan at the other end of the field.

When I was a lad at school my brother Don and I would cycle to Kenley airfield to watch the Hawker Harts and Bristol Bulldogs taking off and landing. We'd park our bikes and lie on the ground at the edge of the field and watch as they soared over our heads. We would talk about aeroplanes and what fun it would be to fly. Today, I doubt if there was a soul who cared what was going on or where we were going. At 5.30 precisely we led the squadron take-off, which from a spectator's viewpoint was no great deal – simply six Beauforts following one another at short

49

intervals into the morning air of the Cornish countryside.

There's nothing to compare with the last-minute preparation, the orderly drill up to the gathering roar of the engines as they are taken up to full power for take-off and the final lurch forward of the aeroplane. Another thing is the smell of an aeroplane (not a modern airliner, naturally). Piston engined military aircraft in particular always have the all-pervading odour of 100-octane fuel. Add to this the scent of various lubricants and, especially at start up, the exhaust gases, and one has an environment which, I think, defies description. It's not objectionable; it's almost homely, something which stays in one's mind for a long time. It's not till the windows are closed and the aircraft gathers speed on take-off that the air clears and all that's left is a memory – as of a fading perfume.

So. Ready to go and time for my usual silent prayer: "Please God take us safely into the air and back to land at the end of our operation".

For take-off the throttles were advanced with considerable caution in order to avoid any swing occurring as we accelerated across the bumpy field. Digger was pretty experienced on this aircraft and *au fait* with most, if not all, of its characteristics, so the trip across the airfield was very orderly. The Observer sat in the second pilot's seat (not that we ever carried a second pilot) for take-off with his feet braced against the base of the instrument panel for there were no straps fitted. Then as the airspeed built up to 100 knots and we became airborne at the second bounce I'd take up my position in the nose. The neat lines of hedgerows beneath us were receding rapidly and the sea came quickly into view. It was calm and there was little wind or drift as we reached 2,000 feet – the altitude for the first leg. It appeared to be getting quite warm when the skipper said that the heating was in one of its "all" positions. That is, it was either all on or all off. Whoever decided to put those heating controls where they were must have had a sense of humour almost as great as the chap who designed them! However, by means of a deft shove with the right foot the status quo was restored.

In company with the other five we were on our way, each to attack one of the destroyers. Or, should we not rendezvous as planned, we would attack the main target itself. Having passed the first heading to the pilot he made a gentle banking turn to port to take us more or less down the coast and overland towards the Lizard. Then we'd fly out to sea before heading in a south-easterly direction from which we would begin our planned interception. By so doing we hoped to have a fair degree of coverage in our search for and interception of our prey. Apart from the occasional fishing vessel there was very little going on. The cloud began to appear and we dropped down beneath it to maintain contact with the sea. Ted, in the turret, could see nothing of the rest of the squadron but we hoped to catch a glimpse of one or two of them as we altered course on to our next heading. Pip, on the other hand, was, as usual, doing his accustomed act of juggling with the coils and checking out the various frequencies. He was quite safe doing this because we would be unlikely to be making any transmissions yet awhile.

There was something special about being airborne. It was exhilarating. As a crew we always adhered to a strict discipline, no talk or chatter except about those things which directly concerned our task in hand. When on long sea patrols I would often have a yen to sing – only to myself, you understand. Should the microphone get itself switched on during one of these sessions one would be left in no doubt whatever by the rest of the crew who were not particularly musically inclined! On this occasion, however, there was not too much time to spare for such luxuries. Digger, on the other hand, seemed to find more solace in a cigarette which, at our altitude, was no problem, for the oxygen mask was usually hanging loose. Whatever we did I'm sure it bore little resemblance to scenes portrayed on films of ops. We just did not chatter or jump up and down with excitement. Most of the conversation concerned headings, distances and times, changes in altitude, airspeed or any other variations which affected the situation. The wireless op would pass me any bearings I might ask for and relay any message he would receive, whilst the air gunner would be left in his solitary splendour of loneliness and discomfort in the turret. We made a point, however, of bringing him into the conversation whenever possible. Fortunately our trips were seldom very long, four or five hours, and it was seldom cold. And if it was, we in the sharp end could always try putting the heating to its 'all-on' position.

We'd been airborne for about an hour and there was still no sign of the rest of the squadron. We were accustomed to operating alone but this time we should have been surrounded by folk we knew. One thought that did strike me, however, was that our compass could be in error, but both the pilot's and mine agreed – and I knew my plotting was correct. Even so, it's a nasty feeling to be the only one in step. If this trip was to be the success we hoped it was imperative that we should all be in approximately the same air space at the same time. Even Digger had a feeling of being alone when he asked me to check our last heading. We came to the conclusion that the others were obscured by the morning mist. We'd surely pick them up later but for the moment their company was rather academic. The cloud was continuing to lower and rain was beginning to splatter the perspex so we went a little lower to get underneath it. There was also a bit of drift which confirmed the met man's forecast of a small front. We altered course to maintain track and increased airspeed to achieve our planned groundspeed. All the while the pilot was flying manually. This was not at all unusual. George was not the most predictable of assistants at the best of times, and at low level he would be an absolute disaster. This meant that this trip, and all like it, was very demanding on the pilot and without accurate flying and close co-operation between pilot and navigator the little mathematical exercises I was hoping to achieve could not possibly succeed.

The weather was definitely deteriorating and getting rather more turbulent. Visibility was now less than a mile but since there was still some time to go to our ETA over the target we were not unduly concerned. Once through this band of turbulence and rain we again entered a comparatively clear patch. Furthermore my calculations showed the wind to be dropping and small patches of low stratus were beginning to appear. As we progressed and neared the target area blankets of sea fog were noticeable. Seeing this, Digger warned the crew to keep a close look-out. There was now only some seven minutes before ETA, we were at around 500 feet and being alternately engulfed in fog and then exposed to clear air.

Two minutes before our ETA there was a call from Ted in the turret to say there were some "large ripples" on the port side. Digger immediately climbed a little and banked to port. Sure enough, between the patches of fog could be seen without any doubt a large ominous wake. And just ahead of this was a huge dark form whose outline was still obscured. Of one thing I was certain: it had to be our quarry. But it was very much larger than I'd expected. Once before, when the *Scharnhorst* was docked at Brest, we'd come pretty close to her when we were laying mines in the harbour. There she looked awfully large. But now . . .

Plotting and log-keeping played no part in what followed: "Bomb doors open", "Arming switches on", I told the pilot as I placed the line of switches on my right to the "on" position. These would withdraw the pins from the safety devices as soon as the mine was released. We were all on the look-out for the rest of the squadron and/or the torpedo squadron who were supposed to have first crack, so to speak.

Normally I'd be manipulating the bombsight by setting on it whatever wind there was, adjusting the height bar to our altimeter height, setting the bombs' terminal velocity, trying to align the verge ring with the compass needle, levelling the bomb-sight and guiding the aircraft onto the target. Keeping 'red on red' was almost impossible to achieve; during evasive action there would be a certain amount of swirl set up in the compass bowl which would give a false reading of our direction. Even the height setting would only be an approximation by virtue of the errors in the aneroid altimeter and not knowing what the barometric pressures were in the area. The only component one could set with any degree of accuracy would be the terminal velocity of the bombs, provided we were high enough. All this I was spared on this occasion for I don't think anyone had bothered to calculate the terminal velocity of a paving stone, for that was the thing to which a land-mine was usually likened. From our altitude the bombsight was almost superfluous, even though there was a device mounted on the drift wires which we were supposed to use for low-level bombing. But we had devised a means of low-level bombing by using marks on the perspex as the foresight and resting the chin on the top of the height bar. Nevertheless we would certainly do our best. There was little point in coming this far only to make a mess of things.

3

The Attack

The *Scharnhorst* was, without doubt, somewhere at the start of the wake we had seen earlier and, no doubt, she would now be aware of our presence both from the noise of our engines and from her radar responses. They could, in all probability, have seen us. With calm deliberation Digger guided the aircraft along the line of the wake as far as I was able to tell him, for the sea was for the most part still shrouded in mist or fog. We gained a little height and were now at a few hundred feet, which, if all went well, would be the height of release of our load. The sea was by this time becoming quite agitated and white foam could be distinguished here and there. Soon there appeared to be a dark area beneath the mist and out ahead, to which I did my best to direct the pilot. Whether this was the *Scharnhorst* or one of the ships escorting her was, at this stage, impossible to tell. Whatever it was we must attack it for the chances of making a second run were a bit slim. The skipper began a gentle turn. We wanted to attack from behind to cross her bows diagonally. Murphy's law dictated otherwise for she was by now completely obscured by fog. In an instant she had disappeared until we were immediately above her bows when she appeared big and large. To release our mine at this point would have meant a large overshoot, so, without another word Digger began to go round again in order to return to where we'd last seen her. For the present she was lost from sight but we continued to turn until we estimated we should be on a parallel track. Sure as eggs we were on a parallel heading, but this time on the ship's starboard side and in a perfectly clear patch of sky. The engines were at full throttle and the props in fine pitch as I began to give the skipper directions for another attempt. We began to turn towards her. Suddenly the aircraft gave a distinct shudder and smoke began to appear from the port engine. There was also some smoke coming from behind the pilot, or so it seemed, as it came into the nose. I was still trying to align the target with the marks on the perspex by giving directions to Digger. But it was soon apparent that things weren't going as they should, for despite my directions, we were turning only slightly and at the same time descending. We had lost our intercom and no amount of turning would enable us to attack on this run either. We would pass way over to starboard. It was at this time that I took a quick peek over my shoulder into the cockpit. We had no communications between us but I could see that Digger had problems as he held the column back and to port. The port engine was still in fine pitch and over-revving as it continued to issue smoke in large quantities.

The skipper must have realized that there was little hope of our being able to reach the target and drop our landmine so at that point he pulled the jettison toggle. The aircraft breathed a sigh of relief as it leapt a few feet into the air before relapsing into its former unhappy state. Although I had a course ready to give the pilot for him to steer to reach home – the normal procedure when leaving the target area – I had my doubts whether Digger could do much about it. What was at once evident was the fact that we were now being hit repeatedly. There was a fire somewhere aft of the main spar, so I collected a fire-extinguisher and went to see. The W/Op's cabin had been badly hit and poor Pip was in a shocking state. He must have been killed in an instant. There was little I could do to help him, so, on impulse, I switched the IFF (Identification Friend or Foe) fully clockwise and clamped the morse key down as we'd been instructed, with the intention of sending a signal which, if base were listening, would alert them to where the target was, or at least enable them to get a bearing. In retrospect, however, I doubt whether any part of the radio was serviceable, for everything seemed such a shambles and Pip was in the middle of it all. I was obviously superfluous there so I attempted to return to the front of the aircraft. From the side window I saw the starboard undercarriage wheel hanging limply down beneath a smoking engine, which, however, was still operating. And Digger was still hauling back on the control column. By this time we were not far off the sea but descending very gently. A lot of wind was finding its way in through the nose, my office, which had been partly shot away. Beyond that point I have no clear recollection of what took place except I remember bracing my feet in the usual way against the instrument panel – the emergency ditching position, or one of them. The optimum position was to brace against the main spar but at this stage of the game that was a long way back. Pip had no longer any need to take such precautions. As for Ted we had no idea how he was faring. In normal circumstances the drill would be "to centralize the turret and pray." Fortunately he had the presence of mind, and the good fortune, to be able to operate the turret manually at just the critical moment to enable him to exit the turret into the sea.

4

Into the Drink

That ditching was something to be wondered at, little short of a miracle. Digger must have used every bit of flying skill he ever possessed to make such a textbook ditching, especially if one takes into account the state of the engines – one on fire and in full power, while the other was seemingly sick and out of control. Into the bargain, he had also collected a certain amount of shrapnel during the process. It can only be assumed that somewhere there was someone keeping a close eye on things.

Everything became very quiet. By God it was quiet after the previous din. Digger was then making his way out through the hatch above his cockpit and I soon followed. The last ridiculous thing I remembered doing before I left was to lift the Syko machine over the side of the depleted nose into the sea! Within seconds of our entering the sea Ted appeared from the turret, having apparently suffered no real harm. The pity was that Pip didn't make it. We had to leave him in the aircraft which with her back broken took no time in sinking, and without trace. The three of us trod water, inflated our Mae Wests and waited for something to happen.

We saw the battleship and some other craft in the distance and we noticed that the *Scharnhorst* even had her gangway down. There was another aircraft somewhere overhead, but it was certainly not a Beaufort. When we did see it we realized it was a Heinkel, probably a 115, and most probably from the *Scharnhorst*. After a while, I do not know how long, there was a largish ship heading towards us. With a few deft movements and with the aid of a sailor wielding a boat-hook in the stern, we were towed away some distance and then hauled aboard, very subdued and full of water. Once aboard we were stood beside what appeared to be a hot boiler and it was not till then that we realized just how cold we were, even though the sea at the end of July is not usually that cold. We were then stripped naked and our uniforms were taken away. There was precious little conversation at this time, but in due course our uniforms, quite surprisingly, were returned to us, a little scorched but dry.

Digger then came once more to the fore. He made the most senior-looking of our captors an offer. He not only suggested but made it very clear to, presumably, the captain of this vessel that he would be handsomely rewarded by the British government if he would be so kind as to take us across the channel to England. This suggestion was not so well received. In fact it was received with some very stern words, which somehow escaped our complete comprehension. But we got the gist especially when he said, "For you the war is over" – an expression we were to hear many times over in the years to come.

This little tale has been told in many words and in retrospect. The formal record by Kapitän zur See Hoffmann, commander of the *Scharnhorst*, gives a more concise account of the encounter, written at the time or very shortly after the event. The only error in this report is the reference to a torpedo. What follows is a direct transcript of the *Scharnhorst's* log obtained from the Air Historical branch, to which I am greatly indebted.

KAPITÄN ZUR SEE HOFFMANN'S REPORT

"Report of the C.O. of the *Scharnhorst*, Kapitän zur See Hoffmann, on the Beaufort torpedo attack on 25 July 1941.

"At 0645 on 25 July 1941 in very misty weather (fog and rain showers) the noise of engines was heard on the port bow, 2½ miles to the south-west of B1 (buoy). Shortly afterwards an aircraft appeared right ahead at a height of about 30 metres and immediately disappeared again into the mist. The aircraft was identified as a Bristol Beaufort, and we could make out the British roundels. Anti-aircraft fire was not possible, owing to the short time the aircraft was in sight.

"At 0700 an aircraft was again sighted, bearing 180 degrees flying away to starboard at a low altitude. It was again identified as a Bristol Beaufort, and the heavy and light flak on the starboard side was locked on to it immediately. The order to fire was given but had to be countermanded as at the same moment an He 115, providing air cover for the ships, and a destroyer were in line of fire. The aircraft, which was not engaged by the destroyer either, disappeared behind the destroyer in the mist.

"At 0705 the Beaufort again re-appeared, bearing 160 degrees and approaching the *Scharnhorst* on a similar course. It was immediately engaged by the whole starboard side armament of:

> 3 twin 105 mm
> 4 twin 37 mm
> 5 20 mm
> 1 quadruple 20 mm flak 35

and brought under effective fire.

"The aircraft was also engaged by the destroyer *Erich Steinbrink* with her light armament.

"The aircraft did not allow itself to be visibly deflected by the AA fire from carrying out its attack, and, when bearing 080 degrees released a torpedo, which bounced off the surface of the water and, while in the air, performed a somersault before disappearing vertically into the water. No torpedo track was seen.

"Before the torpedo was released, three hits with the 37 mm flak and several with the 20 mm were observed from the *Scharnhorst*. One 37 mm shell entered the rear gun turret, one the nose, and one the centre of the fuselage. Right after dropping the torpedo the aircraft attempted to pull up. At that moment the Beaufort received a direct hit with a 105 mm shell from below the rear section of the fuselage, following which there appeared a short tongue of flame and the aircraft, with lowered undercarriage, glided down into the water where it remained briefly afloat before sinking. Shortly prior to hitting the water the descending aircraft was fired at by an He 115 using tracer.

"The aircraft was principally brought down by the 105 mm. The acknowledgement of the shooting down by the *Scharnhorst* and the participation of the *Erich Steinbrink* is therefore proposed.

Ammunition used:

16	105 mm	with time fuse
66	37 mm	with direct action fuse
389	20 mm	

Signed: Hoffmann."

The final record of the day's event was recorded back at St. Eval in the RAF Form 540, the daily record of flights. On the day in question, six aircraft and crews are listed. One aircraft returned to base with an unserviceable turret. Four are stated as having "Duty Performed" but against our aircraft number and crew is written "Failed to Return".

Ah well. We did our best.

Thus began three, nearly four years as guests of the Third and Last Reich.

It was not until 26 December 1943 that *Scharnhorst* met her end off the North Cape of Norway at the hands of the British fleet under command of Admiral Sir Bruce Fraser who later became Lord Fraser of the North Cape.

She had been moved to Norway to operate against the Arctic convoys carrying war supplies to north Russia. Admiral Fraser planned to trap her if she left port; this he did on Christmas day 1943 and with the aid of "Ultra" intelligence he sailed to intercept her as she prepared to attack a north-bound convoy. The *Scharnhorst* had already been driven away by the cruisers *Belfast*, *Sheffield* and *Norfolk* and had turned back only to be confronted by the *Duke of York*. The *Duke of York*, although more heavily armed than the *Scharnhorst*, was slower. *Scharnhorst* was so strongly built that she proved almost impossible to sink. She was probably hit by thirteen 14-inch shells and many 6-inch and 8-inch shells from the cruisers. Admiral Fraser eventually sent his destroyers to finish her with torpedoes. She was holed by eleven torpedoes.

Finally, she appeared to glow red hot from fires raging her whole length and eventually slipped beneath the surface. In the freezing temperatures of the Arctic most of her crew who had survived the action died rapidly from exposure. Only thirty-six of her crew of some 2,000 were rescued.

5

Guests of the Germans

Thus began three years, nine months and some days as a guest of the Germans, known by them as *Kriegsgefangenen* or to ourselves as 'kriegies'. In some ways I like to look back upon that time as my second career for, despite the deprivations and some discomfort, there was much to be learned.

For the most part we were not strictly incarcerated, for incarceration means imprisonment, prison bars and other discomforts. Of course there were times . . . but by and large we had the benefit of the space around our huts in which to walk and exercise and play such games as were available to us, usually as a result of our own ingenuity. Restricted we certainly were as the trip wire marked the limit of our travels. Anyone venturing further was in danger of being shot at by the 'goons' in the observation towers along the perimeter of the area in which we lived. That was clearly defined by a fence of barbed wire and many scrolls of barbed wire in between it and the next barbed wire fence, so that the chance of just jumping over the fence (as some folk at home seemed to think we could have done) didn't really present itself. Mind you, there were many attempts by several inordinately brave types to do so over the years. This, however, is not a tale of escapes and attempts thereat, even though some may get a mention in passing. No, there have been many accounts of escapes attempted, some successful, by those who bravely took part in them. There was also much fiction written on the subject. This, however, will not attempt to vie with fact or fiction; this is just my own personal account of some of the events during my tour of the continent.

Initially, of course, the whole prospect of being pushed around, often at the end of a rifle or machine gun, being encased in a mesh of barbed wire and always under the watchful eyes of the steel-helmeted goons with their searchlights and machine guns in their goon boxes, was somewhat daunting.

One learns, after a while, to concentrate more on living and to ignore, to some extent at least, the unpleasantness of the sur-roundings. One was never alone, although many's the time when a modicum of solitude would have been welcome.

Following our transfer from sea to ship and from ship to shore, we three survivors, Les Collings, Ted Taylor and myself were ushered into a lorry. Our destination was a large barracks inland, somewhere near Brest. Our guards were very well armed but not really unpleasant, even if they didn't seem keen on conversation. Upon our arrival at the barracks Les and I were put in a large room with barred windows and not a great deal of light. But Ted was taken away to join a couple of other types who, we imagined, were in the same situation. (It was the Germans' custom to segre-gate officers and NCOs. NCOs could be made to work outside the camps under supervision whereas officers were not allowed to work). And very soon afterwards Les too was taken off. He was going to hospital, we were told, for he had a heap of shrapnel in his legs. There was just nothing to do except to lie back on the straw palliasse and look at the ceiling and wonder what the score would be. The goon at the door with his rifle beside him didn't offer much comfort either. Such food as there was was pretty unexciting too. It consisted of dry, sawdust-like bread and a bowl of indescribable soup for the main meal. Then there was a meal, which must have been tea; tea there was but it was made from mint leaves and, as such, had little to recommend it in my humble opinion. This was accompanied by a slice of their especially hard bread with a dollop of sweet red 'jam'. At breakfast, however, there was coffee. This was ersatz, of course, and I was reliably informed that it was made from acorns. Nevertheless, it was refreshing and useful for dunking the bread in. Memories of mess meals were becoming quite vivid!

It was to be many months before I saw Les again and Ted eventually moved to a camp next door when I went to Stalag Luft 3. I never saw him but managed to get word of him some time later.

After a couple of days I was joined by two other RAF aircrew and we were transferred by lorry, train and again a lorry to a camp in the middle of nowhere. Here was a fairly large Army contingent and one or two RAF chaps. The weather was good and sunny so that we could laze on the sand (nearly all PoW camps, it seems, were built on sandy wastes) and watch the clouds go by. One of the chaps who had been in this place for some time pointed out to me the outline of the Swiss Alps. There, sure enough, one could see the glint of the sun on the snow-covered peaks through the summer haze. This camp was at Biberach and somewhere out there I realized there must be normality. It looked like an awfully long walk though, but at the same time, this sight instilled a modicum of comfort, especially as there were folk, even then, who were predicting the war's end by Christmas.

The hackneyed expression "university of life" finds ample application in a PoW camp; perhaps "centre of advanced studies" might be more appropriate, for the kinds of thing one learned in a PoW camp were, on the whole, concerned with survival – with a number of embellishments. We were fortunate in that we were, by and large, all of the same age. There were notable exceptions of course; there was, as I learned later, 'Pop' Green for instance who must have been approaching 40. It was said he was the happiest man in a kriegie camp – so happy to be away from his wife – but that's only hearsay! Then there was Ted Chapman (HSL). He must have been in his mid-thirties, approaching forty. He was not aircrew but commanded a High-Speed Launch, the kind used to rescue airmen shot down in the Channel, hence the HSL which he was proud to quote when asked who he was. The great advantage was that we were many and from every kind of calling. There was hardly a trade or profession not represented in any camp. There were lawyers, locksmiths, jackaroos, blacksmiths, bankers, baseball players, engineers, musicians, artists, and of course, professional flyers, RAF and Civil. It was not surprising, therefore, that such potential with so much time at its disposal proved something of a headache to the Germans whose job in life was to keep us confined and from causing too much trouble. There were times when we would bemoan our lot and think we were hard done by but generally we knew we were damned lucky to be alive when so many of our chums didn't make it.

After little more than a weekend in our "villa overlooking Switzerland" the RAF contingent was singled out for a move to no one knew where except the goons, and they weren't telling. Packing was no problem at all. All that one possessed could virtually be carried in the palm of the hand. There was no need to book transport; that had all been arranged and consisted of a tired-looking lorry in the first instance, which conveyed us to a train in a goods siding.

DULAG LUFT

Our destination was Dulag Luft, a transit camp some 10 miles or so from Frankfurt near the village of Oberursel close to the foot of the Taunus Mountains and commanded by one Hauptmann Eberhardt. There were only a handful of us and we were duly escorted from the train along a lane to this new abode. We were immediately 'deloused' – stripped, given a shower – and after a while our clothes were returned to us before we were marched to the camp compound and thence to a cell.

Dulag Luft was run by the Luftwaffe. After the preliminaries we were to discover it to be not an unreasonable place to be as a prisoner (and after considerably more experience of this kind of life in other camps it was a place to look back upon as having been 'comfortable'). In fact it was something of a propaganda machine, about which we were quickly warned by the Senior

British Officer (SBO). For instance, there was the phoney Red Cross man who visited each new arrival in his cell in turn. First came the cigarettes and the cheery greeting followed by a measure of commiseration and then he produced 'the form'. We were required to fill this out with such details as our names, addresses, numbers, next of kin, followed by squadron, aircraft type, details of the operation on which we had been shot down, our base and other 'noncommittal' details! Even to the uninitiated this seemed a bit much and, of course, everyone had been briefed that in the event of being captured we must give only our number, rank and name (all of which were on the 'dog-tags' we wore). The kind gentleman who wanted this information advised us that withholding these 'small details' would prejudice notifying our folks of our survival and the 'good treatment' we were getting. The long and short of all that was when this information was denied him he would collect up his cigarettes saying, "Think it over. I'll come back and see you again". What was surprising at the time, however, was that he already had quite a lot of facts on our particular operation. On reflection the *Scharnhorst* knew jolly well what kind of aircraft we were and may well have identified our squadron code letters (MW) on the fuselage. Whichever way it came about, such details given to people still somewhat bewildered by their radical change of circumstances could but disarm them to some extent. The obvious object of the exercise was to give the impression that most of what was to be known about one was already known, so why be awkward about a few details now?

Whilst at Dulag we were fed reasonably well from Red Cross parcels which went into a communal pool and were distributed as meals from the 'canteen'. Even the Commandant let it be known that we would all be well treated if we behaved ourselves. The war, he said, would soon be over anyway so there was absolutely no point in trying to escape. Furthermore, we may well have the chance to ski in the winter and after the war was over we would all be playing football and cricket together. The Germans playing cricket!! Such thoughts had not really convinced the likes of Douglas Bader, who, with his tin legs, may not have been too frustrated at not being able to play football. So he tried his first escape from here, unsuccessfully as it happened, with the result that the artificial legs, which had been dropped to him by his colleagues from his squadron back in England, were confiscated.

The turnover of kriegies here was quite brisk and our lengths of stay were not long, usually about a week; just long enough for the Germans to pursue their course of interrogation. I met a member of 217 whilst there. His name was Lou Barry and, although I'd not met him before I recalled seeing his photograph back on the squadron. When he died at the age of 82 he was the last surviving professional sculling champion of England. He too was a Navigator and would accumulate some five years PoW time. But he was always cheerful, a fine example to anyone who tended to take this new kind of life too seriously. He was, for instance, one of the worthies who were entrusted by the Germans with the task of sorting out Red Cross and other parcels in the parcels hut for issue to us lesser mortals. One of his duties, from the kriegies' point of view, apart from ensuring the issue of parcels, was to screen the parcels for anything useful to kriegies for potential escape purposes but forbidden by the goons. Lou's swarthy appearance, his deep voice and his hearty chuckle, to say nothing of his cheerful, even happy, demeanour would long be remembered by anyone who knew him.

That was our gentle introduction to *Kriegieschaft*; not unpleasant and sometimes slightly humorous. For instance there was in the field around which we were allowed to walk a goat tethered to a stake. It was not long before someone untethered this creature and allowed it to roam at will around the field. It immediately took great pleasure in charging the first person it spied and sometimes it was the roving goon. The most amusing part were the attempts by the goons to capture the animal. Just good clean fun.

OFLAG XC –Lübeck

Our next port of call was Oflag XC at Lübeck at the south-westerly corner of Schleswig Holstein on the Baltic. This was a different cup of tea entirely – not at all a good spot. The camp was run by the Wehrmacht (Army) who, for some reason, disliked the RAF. Our welcome was what was to become routine on change of camp, a de-lousing. We were stripped of every item of clothing and directed to a primitive shower room. After the shower we stood around to get dry by which time our clothes had been 'deloused' and were returned to us, less anything of value, for which, surprisingly enough, a receipt was given. Some people were even known to get their things back after the war. I was less fortunate for I lost a silver cigarette lighter and a cigarette case. That case, incidentally, may well have saved my life when we got the chop, and I rather treasured it for it had a big deep score mark from corner to corner where perhaps a bullet or a piece of shrapnel had come my way.

We then went to our barracks, which at first sight appeared pleasant enough. They were even surrounded by a kind of lawn and a flower or two could be seen. The huts themselves were brick and painted white, all in good military-style lines. Inside was another matter; there were enough beds to go round, together with a straw palliasse and a blanket each. The huts were divided into rooms with an electric light in the centre above a rectangular table and, to one side, was a cast iron stove for heating. And that was about it. The main problem was the food, or the lack of it, and its quality was nothing to rave about. The daily ration consisted of a can of mint tea which each room collected from the cook-house in a large zinc jug in the morning. Lunch consisted of a bowl of greasy liquid with unknown ingredients floating in it (on one occasion the foreign bodies floating in it were diagnosed as embryo rats) and a fifth of a loaf of hard brown sawdust-laden bread. Grease (or margarine?) together with a can of ersatz jam was issued in bulk weekly to each room according to the numbers of inhabitants in each. Cheating was not possible for to overclaim for one room meant a reduced ration somewhere along the line; the Germans knew precisely how many bodies there were or, on occasions, should have been. Tea consisted of another can of their 'delicious' mint tea with a trace of sweetener.

Treatment by the Germans was brutal at times. Even those officers in the camp hospital received wretched treatment and one actually died of dysentery. In the camp itself we were stood for long periods in the hot sun of summer or the cold of winter as they counted us. On full rations this would have been no problem, but as things were it was all somewhat trying, especially as during this time we were often provoked by the guards, butted with rifles and generally pushed around. One officer, Squadron Leader Roger Bushell, a South African and a one-time British ski champion amongst other things, had the audacity to remonstrate with the Germans during one particularly miserable incident. It made little difference except that he was hit with rifle butts and marched off to the cooler (the gaol in the *Kommandantura*) where he stayed for several days. All in all it was a pretty miserable place. Even so it had its moments. For example, during an air raid one night, a Lancaster which was shot down crashed locally, shedding its bombs as it did so. An incendiary bomb landed in the *Kommandantura* – the German Mess in fact, just on the other side of the wire. It duly caught fire and the guards lost no time in descending upon us to help put out the fire with the aid of the fire hoses in each hut. They connected up the hoses and went back to quell the fire. It just so happened that no water reached the spout of their hoses for mysterious holes appeared along its length. To add to their annoyance we all joined in the chorus "I don't want to set the world on fire" – a popular song about that time. For this we paid the penalty next day. We stood in the sun, being pushed around and threatened, and sometimes hit, with rifle butts for our every movement. But their Mess was a shambles!

Another small incident to relieve the monotony took place when the Commandant's cat strayed through the wire into our compound. One Tony Ruffell, a South African, grabbed poor pussy and almost before you could say knife kitty was in a pot. A brutal incident – and we didn't even enjoy it.

OFLAG VI B – Warburg

At last the time came for us to leave Lübeck. The months had dragged by, broken only by the rare and infrequent arrival of Red Cross parcels. Looking back on that period we were not that dispirited; shall we say we were becoming hardened to that kind of life. Our next 'residence' was Oflag VIb, Warburg near Kassel, west of the River Weser.

This was already an established camp of Army officers, survivors from such places as Dunkirk and St. Valéry. There were some 1000 of them, mainly from the 51st Division, and a pretty spirited lot they were despite their length of time in captivity. They soon befriended us and were only too willing to introduce us to the systems they had evolved. Our contribution was perhaps some new skills to add to theirs, new ideas and, not least, the latest news, as we remembered it, from Blighty. Many of their questions were on subjects about which we had not been too concerned when we were at home; most of them revolved around morale and the public's feeling about the war, in addition to opinions about the effect of air raids and the war at sea. Naturally they were interested to know how the general populace viewed Dunkirk and the shambles which that entailed. This was not really surprising when we came to think about it because their only source of news had been from whatever newspapers the Germans allowed them to see.

Here the huts, each of wood and supported on stilts a couple of feet off the ground, were in two groups. One group, at the far end of the camp and including a brick building originally built as a store for vegetables or animal feed I imagine, adjoined the main gate. Looking out of camp beyond the gate was Desenberg Castle, on a hill. Otherwise in that direction the area was pretty featureless. In front of that was the 'parade ground' or 'football pitch'.

71

At our end there were six or seven huts, wooden as before, the camp hospital, an ablutions block, and the canteen and cookhouse. There was no view from here except for the *Kommandantura* alongside the perimeter wire and, in winter, a sea of mud between the huts. We were accommodated initially twelve to a room which was increased to sixteen as new intakes (which we called 'purges') arrived. Each room had two-tier bunks, a table, a stool apiece and, inside the door, a cast iron stove. These stoves when hot made an excellent toasting machine by sticking slices of bread on the sides. When the bread was done it would simply fall off!

All this was heaven compared with our previous experiences, especially as Red Cross parcels seemed to be arriving fairly regularly, so we ate quite well. We in our room, like many others, decided the best way of going about feeding was to pool any parcels as they arrived and appoint a quartermaster to apportion the rations, including the fifth of a loaf per person per day. Next, a roster of all room members was drawn up to take care of the daily chores of fetching the water, cleaning the room and preparing and cooking the meals. It all worked very well indeed. Any omission by anyone was soon corrected by the many to the satisfaction of all. Certain exceptions were made to the 'stooge' rosters to allow for escaping activities, however – digging holes and the like. Otherwise duties had to be carried out meticulously.

Anything which had to be divided between the sixteen of us had to be done with scrupulous honesty. For instance, the division of a loaf of bread into five equal portions was a fairly tricky business so the procedure went like this. The quartermaster would cut the portions as accurately as he could, then the cards were dealt (having first determined whether aces would be high or low) then the person who drew the highest card would nominate, without looking, the portion he would have. It worked on the principle that no one could be unlucky all his life. So far as Red Cross parcels were concerned it would sometimes become a small problem to divide everything precisely. In such cases the obvious solution was to incorporate these things in a stew or something.

Should there be a small 'residue' the quartermaster could always declare a dividend. The usual practice would be to make a declaration just about the time that everyone was in bed. This would sometimes cause chaos and many a laugh as folk would fall over things in their haste to get first pick. Perhaps such things enabled us to retain our sanity, maybe.

The Army, who'd already had considerably more experience of kriegie life than we, were well organized, in fact very well organized, and had set up an outfit known as 'Foodacco'. There one could, for a small fee, get a wide variety of services such as shoe repairs, tailoring, sewing and darning etc., through cannibalizing existing items. The main business though was the exchange of one portion of food for another. Everything was valued in cigarettes. Prices were clearly marked and accounts were kept. Overdrafts were not normally allowed. The 'jobber's turn' varied a bit but generally it worked out at one percent overall and the proprietors earned their keep. Funnily enough the goons respected this organization and it never came in for too much abuse during 'blitzes'.

After a while the 'Foodacco' idea seemed an idea well worth copying in our room. So Jay (Justin) O'Byrne, a single-engine type from Tasmania, who in later years was to become a senator, and I organized just a small food exchange market, which we called 'The Mart', with a view to providing a feast for the room come Christmas. Our currency was an English biscuit, roughly equivalent to five English cigarettes. Our opening stock we had to borrow from the room – not looked upon with a deal of favour initially. After all, if the idea failed there would be precious little chance of their getting any dividend! It was reasonably successful but nearly came to grief shortly before Christmas when there was a small run on the 'market' and we found ourselves with rather more of the 'exotic' and not enough of the ordinary stock. By and large people still preferred bulk as opposed to luxury foods! But we had quite a 'bash' for our Christmas feast, all done at one per cent. We didn't keep the Mart going long after the New Year; well, for one thing we had a tunnel going in one corner of the

73

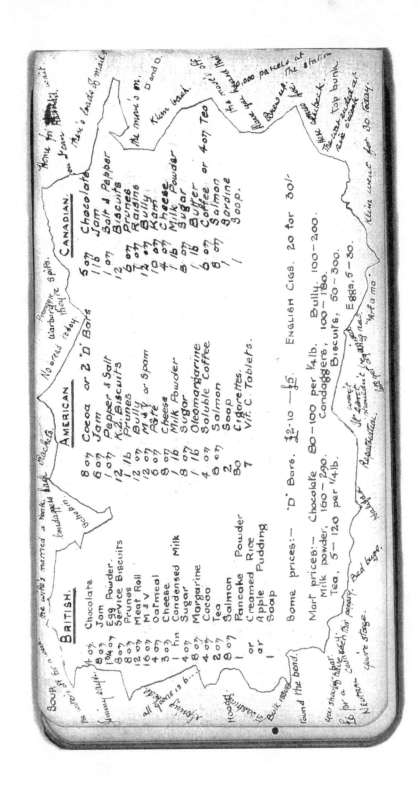

room and it would have been unwise to advertise the fact. Foodacco, however, continued to prosper and to provide a good service for those wishing to use it right up to the time we left the camp on another 'posting' on a bleak mid-winter's night.

The camp was becoming organized in many other respects. Education was beginning to take off; the subjects varied a great deal even if most amounted to little more than talks. But they were popular and, with the arrival of the RAF, their scope was widened considerably. After all there was a wide choice of skills and knowledge represented here. Maybe one didn't envisage becoming a banker, butcher, publican, sheepshearer, jackaroo or a journeyman. But to listen to some backwoodsman of an Australian talking on 'riding the range' and making such digressions as only these people could was a riot in itself. It was an experience to listen to those who had been such things before learning their Service trades. For those few minutes one could leave the realms of PoW camp as the speaker would speak with enthusiasm of his experiences to a bunch of chaps lying around in the sand on a warm summer's day. The more serious lectures were often given in rooms vacated for that purpose by courtesy of the other residents. There were lectures on law, mathematics, astro-navigation, art, languages. Naturally it took some time before the camp was fully organized. But that was about the state of the art when we left many months later.

Then, of course, there were the practical pursuits. These could be divided into two main categories – personal and those 'for the common good'. Personal pursuits would embrace such things as drawing, painting, the making of pots and pans from Red Cross tins, wood carving (the basic material being a bed-board), or even knitting. Pastimes for the common good could be any of these as might be required for escape. Here the chap handy with a piece of wood could manufacture items for use in a tunnel; the artistic might employ some of his talents in map-making or preparing documents; the potential tinsmith would find ample application in making items for tunnels, such as compasses or parts for an air pump. There was much scope for dexterity and/or imagination.

In the early days I recall helping to make condensers (or, in modern parlance, capacitors) for the radio. The radio wizards would calculate the requirements and the artisan would manufacture the goods. Capacitors weren't difficult to make. It required tin-foil from cigarette packets (and it really was tin in the British cigarette packet) and dehydrated grease from the rations, into which suitable toilet paper was dipped to make the dielectric. When placed together, alternately tin-foil/greased paper, in the number and size determined by the 'experts' and carefully joined together at their opposite ends, this produced a capacitor of the required capacity.

This is but one example of useful things a bright boy could do! Others included the noble art of cutting glass with a pair of nail scissors under water (useful when making compasses), making sticks of solder out of tin-foil from cigarette packets and many other little tricks born of necessity.

Naturally, life was not all that placid all the while. There were always the Germans to contend with. They often liked to disrupt whatever it was we were doing. Perhaps it was their suspicious minds which caused so many interruptions, especially after an escape attempt had been thwarted or another tunnel had been found or some incriminating evidence had come to light. In most camps though, I think they worked on the principle that if we were playing games, listening to or giving talks or drawing pictures we couldn't be getting up to too much mischief! So we did all these things in order that everyone could be happy! Block, or even whole camp, searches was common practice. They usually happened at the time of the morning *Appell*, when the usual contingent of guards was followed a few minutes later by a larger bunch who would station themselves around a particular hut or take over the whole camp – whilst we were herded together to be counted. It was quite amazing how often the Germans found it necessary to count us and, for that matter, how long they would take! The duration of a search depended on what they thought they were looking for and how successful they were in finding it. Inevitably we suffered to a greater or lesser extent. Most often everything we owned was strewn on the floor or, not infrequently, thrown out of the windows into the mud or the snow or, in the fine weather, just distributed liberally abroad. Meanwhile we had little option but to stand around in whatever weather the good Lord had provided. On occasions when just one block was being searched the rest of the camp would provide a brew of something or other, hot in winter and cool in summer, for 'the sufferers'. This seemed to annoy the Germans who found it difficult to prevent entirely and who themselves were not so well catered for. This procedure was commonplace.

I have many memories of VI B, the most prominent of which are the happier ones. I recall, for instance, quite vividly the concert given by the camp orchestra. It was an orchestra composed mainly of Army personnel but included Larry Slattery, one of the earliest Air Force kriegies. It was a concert of classical music which included Mozart's piano concerto number 23 in D. The concert hall was the canteen/dining room (not that it was ever used by us as such) but that was its name. I suppose a hundred or more at a time could pack themselves into it, each one carrying a stool from his room. And those who could not get in would sit outside to listen. Even some of the German officers came across for the event. Maybe they wanted to assure themselves that the musical instruments which had been allowed from the Red Cross or YMCA in the very early days, or may even have been purchased from the Germans, were not being misused. It was a wonderful concert. We also had several stage productions by the theatrical crowd. These were encouraged by the Germans. If a Shakespeare play were being put on the Germans were always keen to "be invited". Again, because they felt such activities were harmless they tended to encourage them by providing material like Red Cross crates for our use – on parole, of course. In the summer of that year the Army put on a gala garden party in which various folk dressed up as women (and some quite attractive at that) would parade around the camp on improvised floats, whilst, at the same time there would be singing and competitions. The day, as I recall it, was pretty hot and almost everyone joined in this frivolity until the place seemed more like a small fairground than a kriegie camp.

Then, one day, there was the visiting general who decided he would do the thing in style and drive into camp with an escort on foot and pay a call on the Senior British Officer. It just so happened that while he was paying his social call a lot of people gathered around his car, which was guarded by his chauffeur and a goon. While uttering expressions of admiration others were helping themselves to small attachments here and there. On the General's return these discrepancies were noted whereat the General had to return to the SBO to 'ask' that the missing items be returned forthwith. As the SBO explained, it was all a joke really but that, in due course, everything would be restored to its rightful owner. It would take time, however, because, as the General himself would appreciate, communications in the camp were not all that good. Well, in due course everything (almost) was restored and a very boot-faced senior German officer left after some delay and amidst a resounding cheer from all present. There were so many truly amusing incidents. I say truly amusing; they were to us at the time for we tended to derive great pleasure from the simplest and silliest of events.

There were many of us in this camp, as I've mentioned, and not unnaturally we had slightly different views on some matters. For instance, the Army was proud of its discipline and its turn-out on parade and this was their way of showing the Germans that, kriegies or not, they were quite capable of maintaining their high standard of discipline. So when it came to *Appell* time, especially the early morning one, they would all be booted and spurred in reasonable gear and would drill as they had always done. This, however, was not the RAF's custom. We would invariably arrive late and dressed in the worst clothes we could muster. Instead of standing in neat ranks and files of five from which we could easily be counted we somehow got a bit mixed up. Smoking on *Appell* was forbidden by the Germans, so we smoked. In fact we were quite shambolic. We paid the penalty by having to stay 'on parade' far longer than would normally be the case. The object, however, was to make life just that little more tedious for the Germans by whatever means. Come the King's birthday, however, we'd arrive on parade five minutes early, we'd be drilled by our separate block commander and called to attention. The order was then "Gentlemen, today is the birthday of His Majesty. Three cheers for His Majesty". And with that we'd doff our head-gear and give three of the most rousing cheers imaginable. We'd then be ordered to replace our headgear and we'd be dismissed and return to our huts, change from our gents' natty uniforms (or what had once been uniforms) and again go out for *Appell* in our accustomed scruffy manner. The German officer accompanied by his NCO would then come onto the 'parade ground', salute the senior kriegie officer and say, "*Guten Morgen meine Herren*", to which we'd all reply something to the effect of "go away". The counting could then begin.

One far from funny event was a tragedy in a tunnel from the canteen. The team involved were not aware of the presence of electrical power cables until too late and the unfortunate tunneller was electrocuted. For this we had to ask the Germans to help us by turning off the power supply at that point. They finally did this, of course, but they were altogether mystified by the request and it was not till we'd all been on parade again to be counted that things returned to normal.

One of the pastimes of many of us was the collection of the small pieces of coal or coke which could be found on the parade ground and paths in camp and you'd often see characters lying on the ground picking up these gems and placing them carefully in tins. These little pieces of coal, cinders or whatever, could be burned in the home-made tin stoves for heating water for brews.

It was at Warburg that the Germans started to read out a warning to the effect that "Any British officer incompetently approaching a German Vemmin will be shot". This always raised cheers and hoots of laughter, so much so that they didn't persist too long with their warning. Most announcements were treated with the same disdain.

After some months we had to move again, at least the RAF

contingent had to move. We were beginning to feel like nomads as we packed our worldly possessions and set off for, to us, another unknown destination. Such moves always happened at night under a blaze of searchlights accompanied by the shouting of the guards and much confusion. Mind you we didn't do much to help either. Then began the long trek to the station or should I say siding, for kriegies always seem to entrain in sidings. Maybe it was that sidings were always better lit than the stations. And another point, sidings could accommodate more cattle wagons than stations could! I never realized just how difficult it must have been to count people as they climbed aboard these wagons. But the Germans always had great difficulty! Furthermore, it would have been hard to escape when one considers that the whole area was surrounded with bolt-clicking rifles at the ready. Eventually, amidst much pushing and shunting by the engine, we would get under way, huddled together, some forty or more of us per wagon on a distinctly non-sight-seeing trip to our next camp. A long journey indeed.

OFLAG XXI B –Schubin, Poland

After a most uncomfortable journey we arrived at another goods siding onto which we were off-loaded with little decorum to set out along a small lane, heavily escorted, into the blackness and wetness of the night. This was Schubin, near Poznan, east of the Oder. It was certainly nice to stretch our legs again and to breathe the cleaner air and, sure enough, we arrived. No great welcome, just another search before being directed to a series of low, long, red-brick buildings on the side of a hill. This was to be communal living of a high order – just one long building with a number of two- and three-tiered bunks, some tables and a few stools. As usual, though, we soon settled in and managed to join with our particular chums for the most part. There was obviously no great degree of comfort to be found in this place but things would soon fall into position and were bound to look better in the cold light of morning. Meanwhile we would just throw ourselves on whatever bunk came readily to hand and call it a day.

The morning dawned all too soon as we were herded out onto the area adjoining the huts to be counted. There we could see the usual parade ground-cum-*sportsplatz* and alongside was an area which at some stage must have been a garden. I don't know who the previous occupants were – we were told they were French – but whoever they were they were a mighty untidy lot; one might go so far as to say scruffy. There was rubbish, and, would you believe, bottles everywhere! This place was cold, wet and totally uninviting. However, the first thing was to get properly cleaned up after our journey. This we were able to do in the ablutions which were situated in the centre section of each long hut. This particular facility was seldom difficult to locate since it was invariably awash from the overflowing troughs and the blocked drains. In the height of summer, however, things looked a whole lot better, but much less useful because, most times, there was precious little water. The trick here, and at subsequent camps, was to get to the ablutions block fairly early, collect a jug of water from the tap and pour it into a large tin with holes drilled in the base. This would then be suspended by a chum so that we could take it in turn to get a shower.

In no time at all we had the place organized. From an area of apparent dereliction outside the block in which we were, we found pieces of bent ironwork and a number of dilapidated house bricks from which we built cooking stoves. Some of these were quite sophisticated. Ours for instance had a chimney, which improved the draught. The surface above the fire was for the cooking whilst at the sides we had an oven to keep things warm. And it all worked, driven by pieces of bedboards, clinker/coal from the paths and anything combustible. Some worked better than others but whatever happened we all generated a lot of smoke from the rather dubious fuel at our disposal.

In the huts a code of conduct evolved, not unnaturally concerning the amount of noise generated. Since there were no walls to divide these barracks noise travelled easily. During the day most people would be outside if the weather were reasonable. But, come locking-up time up to a hundred folk, usually wearing clogs and tramping around on a concrete floor, provided the general background noise to the buzz of conversation. Heated discussion, for instance, was for everyone's enjoyment or displeasure. We were a pretty tolerant lot though.

At the end of our particular part of the barrack and in the opposite corner was a mixed group of about a dozen Australians and New Zealanders, a couple of Canadians and some British (or Poms!). Among them was a raconteur, a storyteller of no mean repute who, some nights after lights out, would invent some tale or other usually woven around some of the better known characters in the block. He would begin one of his famous tales and, to give you some idea of their quality, hardly a soul raised any objection. In fact no one was asked; these sessions just began and by the time they ended most people were asleep! Even if I were able to remember any of those yarns now I couldn't hope to emulate either the person telling them or the manner in which they were told. I don't know what happened to him, but I wouldn't mind betting that, should he have ventured into print, he could have made a fortune. On the other hand, what amused us then may not have had the same effect on folk today. We even took delight in recalling our own simplicity.

We also thought it amusing whilst 'on parade' being counted during the summer months to catch some of the flies (and there were plenty in this rural area) and to attach a length of unravelled cotton with a small paper drogue at its end to the leg of the unfortunate fly. This creature and many of his friends would then fly around ourselves and the goons who were trying to count us. This at first annoyed the Germans who of course forbade the practice. Eventually, however, they tried to ignore our little prank and from time to time, in an unguarded moment, would even be seen to smile.

They didn't smile so readily when some thirty or more were missing from the morning *Appell*. From the 'abort,' or loo block, across the 'parade ground' a tunnel had been dug and after some

82

months of hard work by that particular party, it was broken into the adjoining field. I think a couple of chaps reached home as the result of it and it caused considerable uproar amongst the goons, so much so that the Gestapo was brought in on the act. They naturally searched the whole camp but found comparatively little. Each bod was taken aside into the barrack and searched. Now there was a waste of time! Come the time for them to depart, however, there was more consternation. For it was at that point they found they were short of one beautiful black leather coat and a pair of gloves. These articles soon reappeared when they began the traditional shouting and brandishing of guns. After all they were of limited value to us. There were few who would have relished being caught in an attempt to get home wearing the hallmark of the Gestapo.

It was at Schubin that the Germans decided I should do my stint in the cooler. Way back in the distant past whilst at Warburg I was unfortunate enough to be caught down a hole, en route to Switzerland! The idea had been to surface somewhere in an adjoining cornfield but the best-laid plans somehow went awry and we broke out into the path taken by the goons who patrolled outside the wire. So instead of looking up at the clear blue sky I found myself at the wrong end of a rifle! It just so happened that the coolers were already full and my custodial sentence had to be delayed. But it caught up with me at Schubin, in the middle of the winter. Now this was no bad thing, even though coolers were not meant to be comfortable. They were quiet. Solitude is one of those things seldom encountered in *kriegieschaft*. All that and a single room to boot! Cigarettes were *streng verboten* but it was not difficult to overcome this to a small extent. And for those who couldn't manage it there were numerous messages in morse around the wall to tell one where they could be found, usually along the ledge at the top of one of the walls. I spent twelve glorious days there and even had a good soup once a day in addition to the normal fifth of a loaf. The soup, as always, was prepared under German supervision by the British who, when it came to providing the ration for the chaps in the cooler, usually managed to apportion a little more of the solid and less of the liquid, which was mostly water anyway. Living under these circumstances was easy; no *Appells*, no standing around in the snow waiting to be counted. This kind of punishment I could endure for a long time, but then I should only be depriving others who were waiting their turn! Seriously though, I had been lucky again for life in the cooler in other camps was not so inviting – Lübeck, for example.

Attempts to escape were the order of the day and in every which way, so the Germans used every method to dissuade such goings on. As a possible last resort they put, so they told us, land mines along the perimeter between the trip wire and the fence proper. During this time I was busy making compasses and drawing maps of the area copied from scraps we had come by. For exercise there was the usual circuit pounding. Come the winter when the snows and frost came we had no problem in making an ice-rink. This was done by carrying out buckets and cans of water and pouring them onto the ground where they froze in a very short time. Surprisingly enough, the Germans provided a number of pairs of skates. They were somewhat down at heel and not *à la mode*, but they provided a great deal of pleasure.

Christmas was, in its way, quite a festive season, not that it involved presents or, for that matter, decorations. But we always managed to have a little spare food in the kitty even if we had no 'Mart' with which to augment our reserves. To offset any deficiencies we in our syndicate had been putting any excess dried fruit from our parcels into a bucket with a little water in it. With the addition of a couple of scrounged yeast tablets we managed to produce a kind of fermented mess. When carefully strained, not necessarily through an old sock but through a piece of cloth and flavoured with whatever came to hand, we had a passable brew. Perhaps the imagination played a part in our enjoyment as we toasted one another, reckoned ourselves lucky and drank to our chums back home.

As a concession the Germans allowed us a little extra freedom at Christmas by leaving the doors unlocked so as to permit us to visit between blocks after dark. Normally we'd be locked in at night. That Christmas in Poland I remember so well; it was pretty darned cold, the snow underfoot squeaked as one walked and the stars shone brilliantly. I decided to take a short stroll down to the 'ice rink' just below the barracks. There were so many things flashing through my mind at this time: my parents, my brother and sister and many friends back home to say nothing of the chums I'd made during training and on the Squadron. Christmas is a time for remembrance.

As I approached I could see a goon stamping up and down along the outside of the wire occasionally stopping to beat his arms across his body to get warm. Then he began singing quietly to himself *Heilige Nacht*. Not to be outdone he was joined by the chap in the goon-box on the corner. The sound of their singing, the noise of boots on the snow and the reflection of the perimeter lights off the snow was something to be wondered at and did more to revive memories of Christmases long ago than I'd ever imagined. There was something magical about that night. Those chaps were probably a whole lot colder than I. They were people (just for a few moments), and they, like as not, believed in the same God as I and had loved ones somewhere or other with whom they'd rather be than doing what they were doing just now. I felt so good I could have wished them a Happy Christmas. Yes, I hoped they would have a Happy Christmas.

Once again the time had come for yet another move. Rumours had been rife for some time. Not that we could do much about it when the time came except to resist any temptation to eat whatever chocolate our parcels might provide and to conserve it for possibly harder times. Even so we were ready when the move was finally announced and, by and large, we would not be sorry to move on. It would be a new experience; no doubt it would be *quite* a new experience.

STALAG LUFT III –Sagan

Our arrival at Stalag Luft 3, 100 miles or so south-east of Berlin, was a very orderly affair. The doors of the cattle wagons were dragged back to the shout of the goons saying, '*Aus, Raus*' in their customary manner. And there appeared to be even more guards there to welcome us at this goods siding than usual. There was a lot of discussion between the German officers and between our officers and NCOs; feet were stamping and rifle bolts were clicking. Eventually we all moved off towards the camp. As usual it was a fairly flat area in what appeared to be a series of pine forests. Of course we were searched before being channelled outside the search hut to await the completion of this tedious process. Eventually down to the camp we went and there was a lot of camp. We went to what was known as the East Camp – implying that there must be a North, South and West. Sure enough, as we discovered later, there were. East Camp looked fairly, but not quite, new. In the area surrounding the huts, of which there were two rows of four, tree stumps seemed to abound. So it was a fairly new camp.

The SBO was Group Captain 'Dickie' Kellett, who in 1938 had flown non-stop from Egypt to Australia – a quiet, unassuming chap.

As usual we had banded ourselves into groups of particular buddies so that when we were counted in through the main gate we could head for a room and there take up residence. Beds were allocated strictly on the basis of first come first served. But there was a bed apiece in two-tier bunks as usual. Each bed had its allocation of bed-boards, ten to a bed. These formed the base of the bed and extended crossways in the frame on which the palliasse rested. The rooms were intended for between twelve and sixteen, i.e. there was room for expansion! It just so happened that I was in a room of Australians. It was simply the way things worked out, but I couldn't have chosen a better bunch. They came from all parts of Australia and had, pre-war, been employed in almost every kind of activity. There was a school master, a professional cricketer, a jackaroo (a worker on a sheep station), a bank clerk, a sheep shearer, a local government chap and a Tasmanian, Jay O'Byrne (We ran the 'Mart' back at Warburg. It was from him that I learned how to cut hair, sheep-shearing fashion I think) and others of the same ilk. Almost without exception, they were comedians – or so it seemed to me at the time. We all got along pretty well, even heated discussions dissolved sooner or later in a hoot of laughter. Les Dixon, the cricketer, and I got along well and many's the circuit we did together. Their aircraft had been badly damaged by flak but he had managed to fly it back as far as the English Channel before it crashed. Most of the crew had got out into a dinghy. Unfortunately he drifted to within sight of the English coast and back again before being picked up by a German launch. By coincidence we shared the same birthday. Such was my original lodging at Luft 3.

Stalag Luft 3 East Camp embodied everything we had previously encountered, except that the good things seemed better and the not so good weren't so bad. It was filled entirely by RAF aircrew (or, to be more precise, aircrew from many of the Allies), with the exception of a few folk who were ground specialists and had also been captured. As ever the camp was built on sand and apart from where it adjoined another compound it looked out onto a pine forest. In this respect it must have been a fairly healthy spot! The huts were on stilts as usual which enabled the 'ferrets' to crawl underneath and to make tunnelling a little more difficult.

I was in block 64 where the block commander was 'Wings' Maw. He and Squadron Leader Sargent occupied the room at the far end and between them they had an 'engineering workshop' where they made things from iron into useful items for tunnelling. They also built themselves an air-conditioning system which opened the window at night should it become too hot and which closed again when necessary. To achieve this they had to drill a couple of holes in the floor. It was not long before the visiting 'ferret' (the goon who would often station himself under the hut at night to eavesdrop and to watch for tunnellers) found this hole.

It seemed natural enough for him to stick his finger into this. Wings Maw, quick as a flash, managed to put his foot neatly on to the intruding finger. I believe he did a stint in the cooler as a result!

The camp, or rather its inmates, again sported virtually every kind of activity. Formal lectures were organized; one could undertake a wide variety of studies, even sit some examinations. There was considerable scope for the arts in that we were allowed, even encouraged, to build a theatre with paroled material in one of the rooms. It just so happened that this room was next to ours so we could always have a preview of any production through a hole we made in the wall. We played a lot of sport; this was mainly softball or 'golf' in the summer, and football. We also had a sports day and crazy days when, for bets, folk would push a ball around the 'circuit' with their noses! People made things from the tins contained in Red Cross parcels, and when there was absolutely nothing else which appealed at the time one could pound the circuit – that was the usual form of exercise. (It was interesting to note that circuits were invariably done anti-clockwise; in fact it was distinctly strange to walk the other way round.) All in all this was the best organized and least miserable of all the places we had so far visited. But it had its unpleasant side as well when the Germans became really upset, for the number of escape attempts must have been greater than from any other camp.

But before anyone gets the impression that life was simply one big picnic with nothing to do but await the war's end perhaps I should elaborate. One, if not the only, aim was to cause the Germans as much trouble as possible and by so doing to cause them to retain the maximum number of guards to keep us in order; escape attempts assisted this aim. Most people, therefore, were engaged for some of their time in some nefarious activity. Every attempt to gain the wide open spaces was carefully organized and administered, mainly to prevent one attempt prejudicing another. So although many tunnels were dug they were seldom dug indiscriminately. They were co-ordinated. Furthermore, resources had to be carefully allocated to provide

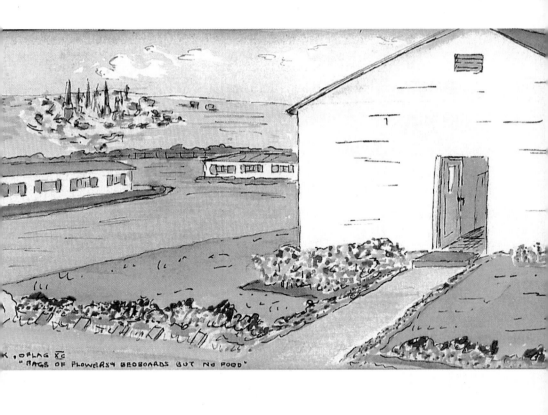

K. OFLAG XC
"BAGS OF FLOWERS, BEDBOARDS BUT NO FOOD"

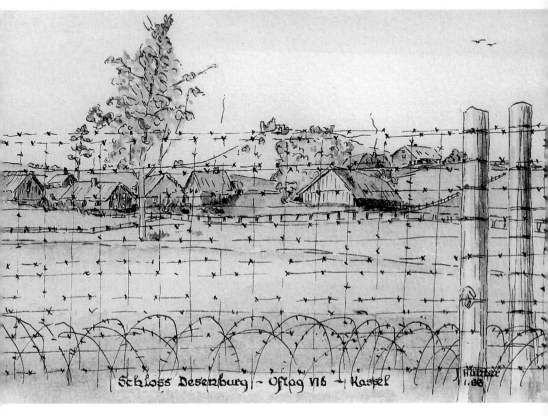

Schloss Desenburg - Oflag VIB - Kastel
Hutter
1.88

East end.   West end.

VICTORY
AND HOW.

Schubin – Cooler.   Feb. 10. '43.   Cooler – Fothe

"COOLER SPORTPLATZ."   FEB. '43.

ICE RINK — FROM OUR WINDOW.

WASH ROOM (BATH ROOM) XXIB

Schubin. '43. Kriegie-made cooking stoves.   Necessity the mother of invention! I'll say!

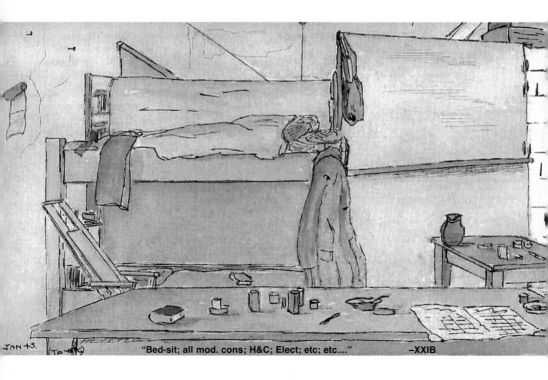

Jan '43.   "Bed-sit; all mod. cons; H&C; Elect; etc; etc...."   —XXIB

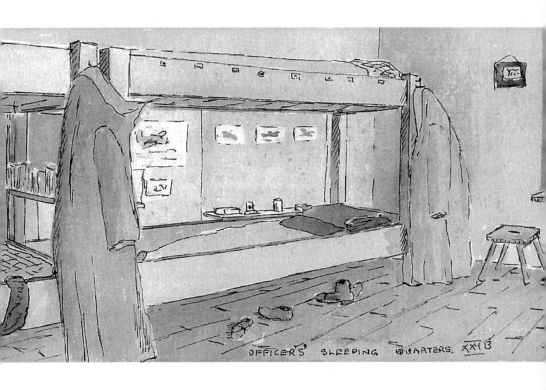

OFFICERS' SLEEPING QUARTERS. XXIB

N.C.O's Compound Sagan

Room 6 Bk. 64. Sagan.

LOOKING NORTH FROM Bk. 64. SAGAN.

THE CHADWICK, HUNTER CORNER. SAGAN.
Bk 64 Rm. 6.

Main Gate. (looking N.E).   Sagan (Stalag Luft 3)   Sept. 44.

THE GARDEN FROM WINDOW.

SAGAN
MAY 44.

"ANY EVENING, ANY DAY." BK 64-6.

those who were considered to have the best chance of success a better share of whatever was available. Or again, we could lay on a sport or activity to divert attention from someone wishing to crawl under the wire, or along a drainage ditch for instance. An example of this took place at VIB, Warburg, when two chaps from our room decided to try crawling along a drainage ditch near the main gate. There was a goon-box nearby and the usual patrolling guard along the perimeter fence, so we organized a mud fight on our side of the wire just below the goon-box. This was done amidst a lot of shouting and, to an extent, rolling in the mud as we 'fought'. This distraction was only fairly successful as our two chums were spotted shortly afterwards.

The theatre, the props and even the seats were constructed from the crates in which Red Cross parcels arrived. Of course these things and the tools for the job were on loan from the Germans strictly on parole. We were always meticulous in the honouring of our word and they knew it. There was, I believe, a wealth of talent among us so that many a good play or a review could be seemingly professionally performed. Stafford (Aidan) Crawley could provide an entertaining song-and-dance act, Rupert Davies often took the lead roles in the more serious plays. One show which appealed to me particularly was Thornton Wilder's *Our Town*. There was also a kind of variety act which, with the aid of a band, proved quite successful. In this appeared a down-at-heel, dishevelled character who just stood with his hands deep in his pockets and recited:

Bloody life is bloody hard, bloody wire, bloody guard,
Bloody dogs in bloody yard, bloody, bloody, bloody.
Bloody icerink's bloody mud, bloody skates no bloody
    good,
Sat where once I bloody stood, bloody, etc.
Bloody bridge all bloody day, learning how to bloody play,
Bloody Blackwood's bloody way, bloody, etc.
Now and then, though bloody stale, censor brings in bloody
    mail,

Better draw the bloody veil; bloody, etc.
Bloody girlfriend drops you flat, like a dog on bloody mat,
Gets a Yank like bloody that; bloody, etc.
Bloody sawdust in the bread, must have come from bloody
    bed,
Better all be bloody dead, bloody, etc.
Don't it get yer bloody goat? Was it Shaw who bloody
    wrote,
Where the hell's that bloody boat? Bloody, etc.
Now I've reached the bloody end, nearly round the bloody
    bend.
That's the general bloody trend. Bloody, etc.

In addition to the theatre we occasionally had a 'music night'. That was when our turn came to use the camp gramophone in our hut. This, naturally enough, was a wind-up machine playing 78 rpm records. The gramophone was supplied by the Red Cross, (or was it the YMCA?) in the early days; records came from several sources, sometimes from the Red Cross, sometimes from individuals. I personally got several through the Canadian Red Cross from a group of ladies at Swift Current, Saskatoon, a place I'd never previously heard of. In fact it may have been one Eddie Assilan, a Canadian I knew, who may have instigated this. This was a very pleasant surprise which, in response to my 'thank you' card, produced several letters telling me of life in their big, wide-open spaces. However, with the aid of a volunteer, and there was never any shortage, selected records would be played after lights out from the hut corridor for all to enjoy. It was a pretty cold and draughty job sitting out there I can assure you, but so worth-while. I remember so well my particular favourites. They were Esther Rothy and the Vienna Philharmonic Orchestra playing Franz Lehar's '*Meine Lippen sie küssen so heiss*' and '*Liebe du Himmel auf Erden*'. Others included Tschaikowski's '*Waltzer aus der Serenade*' and some piano music played by Carmen Cavallero 'You are too beautiful' and 'The most beautiful girl in the world'. Generally, we enjoyed almost any music. Obviously the choice was not great but practically everyone enjoyed what we had. I can so well recall my favourites.

In order to keep tabs on the movement of the goons as they came into camp we had a 'duty pilot' – a kind of duty officer. A roster was prepared to provide a look-out from the window of a hut nearest the main gate and from there to log the arrival, movements and departure of any German coming into the camp. This was done quite overtly, so much so that the Germans themselves made use of our services and would, from time to time enquire of the duty pilot where one of their colleagues was. It was necessary to employ people to 'keep cave' for activities wherever they were taking place. Just because a chap was sitting on the steps of a hut contemplating his navel didn't mean he had nothing better to do. He would be keeping a very close watch indeed for the approach of any goon. Communications were quite rapid when necessary. Should a German choose to wander through a block at any time, even though nothing much might be going on, the cry 'goon in the block' would be shouted by the first person to spot him.

These services were never more required than when the 'canary' squawked or 'Jimmy' was on. This was the almost daily news service provided by a small and very select band of worthies who worked the radio, listened to the news and transcribed it for general dissemination. This was of immense value to us all. Without it we would have a very distorted view of the war's progress and so it had to be given special protection in every stage. My friend Lou Barry, mentioned at Dulag Luft, was a leading light in this field, for which he was awarded the MBE at the war's end. The concealment of the equipment was of paramount importance and was achieved in many ingenious ways. One of the most original probably was by concealing it behind a wall which had been moved in its entirety to leave sufficient space behind for the equipment without betraying the fact that the room was just that little bit smaller! We sometimes had the feeling the Germans knew we had a radio somewhere. They would search a hut quite suddenly and, so far as we could estimate, without any reason. I believe, however, that a friendly goon would sometimes give us the wink when a serious search was imminent. But to continue the saga of 'Jimmy': almost from the beginning of my *kriegie-schaft*, certainly from Warburg, we had a fairly regular news service. At Luft 3 there was hardly a day when we had no news, even if sometimes it had to be curtailed due to security difficulties. We even had news during the march when we left Sagan. Next door to us was the NCOs' compound and, although we could barely see over the wire and fence which separated us, we were able to keep them in touch with the news from 'Jimmy' by placing the paper in a small tin and throwing it over the fence to them. The time and place of so doing had to be carefully chosen!

Perhaps my greatest surprise and possibly the highlight of my life at Luft 3 (or any other camp for that matter) came about one summer's day on the arrival of a new purge (the arrival of a batch of new kriegies). As the war progressed more PoWs would arrive. As usual I went to the main gate to see if, just by the off-chance, there was anyone there I knew. To date I'd found no one, which was not surprising since we flew mainly over water and survivors were few. I did notice, however, one character in the line-up who was heavily bearded and wore a white woollen hat. He looked as though he might know me but I couldn't then reciprocate and I left things at that. After completing my circuit I went back to my room in block 64 and sometime later there was a knock at the door which I went to answer. At first sight there was no one there until I looked down to find this chap on his knees. The first words he said were, "Renie Eglinton". At once I knew who he was. It was my old 'rival' Roger Simmons. I say 'rival' for I never knew the chap apart, that is, from the fact that we had similar tastes and 'shared' the same girl when we were both at school, he at John Ruskin and I at Caterham, way back in the mid-thirties. Discipline in the home was rather more strict then than today; we both had our domestic chores to attend to and school homework to complete before we were allowed out – and then only one evening a week, apart from choir practice. My evening was on Thursday and Roger's was Tuesday, or was it the other way round? The deadline in each case was nine o'clock!

Roger was flying Spitfires with No.1 (South Africa) Squadron when he was shot down in the desert. He had a miraculous escape for a shell had struck the armour-plating at the back of his seat and thrust a bolt from it into the back of his head. He didn't know how he left the aircraft, but he landed safely by parachute. Also, he was fortunate that his captors took him in a short time to hospital where they performed the necessary operation to remove the offending bolt. That, as he explained, was the reason for the white woolly hat he wore!

Roger moved into the 'flagship', block 62, the block in which lived the SBO and his 'staff'. I lived in the next block, number 64. It wasn't long, however, before we were comparing notes on our private lives and also the camp routine in which I could give Roger the general rundown. The great thing was that from that time on I had a real friend. After all, before the war we had lived within a mile or so of each other and so could discuss things and places and people we both knew. Another thing: we had both been members of the same Boys' Club, but we hadn't known one another personally. I suppose we each had our own group of friends and since time is infinite in youth we'd no doubt we'd come across each other in some sport or other, sometime. What was apparent was that neither he nor I had any contact with our erstwhile mutual girl, Renie. Roger was at the time engaged to Iris, whom I'd not met, and I'd lost touch with Renie when we both started work.

This camp, run by the Luftwaffe, seemed more orderly than any previous camp; rations, much the same as elsewhere, came up more or less on time and even Red Cross parcels were issued on time as a rule. There were stoppages, of course, and there were restrictions on how they would be issued on account of some misdemeanour or other. Restrictions could be that all tins had to be emptied into containers so as to deprive us of the use of the tins themselves. Can you imagine prunes, sardines and creamed rice or some other mixture all together on the same plate? Plates were scarce! Or sometimes certain things were withheld. Such things were irritating rather than harmful. Another factor was the more frequent arrival of mail, which despite the news it would sometimes convey, did so much to maintain morale. The Germans here knew that the RAF was a pretty dedicated service; dedicated, that is, to the persistent idea of trying to get home and to trying to pin down as many guards as possible in attempting to prevent us. So they did what they considered necessary to thwart our attempts. Overall, I think we were reasonably successful.

After my earlier attempts I decided that digging holes in the sand with the risk of the whole lot caving in on one was not my forte. Instead I joined a small team of two who traded under the name of Dean and Dawson. Dean and Dawson was the name of a travel agency which operated in the City of London. Our specialization was forgery. We operated in what was laughingly known as the canteen, a large dining room and kitchen. It was from here that the daily soup ration was issued in bulk but few, if any, would eat in the 'dining room'. We had a small room at the back, which sometimes doubled as a 'reading room'. There we were able to operate under the noses of the Germans in the adjoining goon-box and those in the kitchen. Outside the window, in the space between the canteen and the perimeter wire, the renowned 'Wooden Horse' operated. Now forging was one way of getting on the escape list. That is, not everyone could or for that matter wanted to dig tunnels and, since there were so many allied tasks associated with getting out of camp, those taking part in, for example, forging, were allocated a slot on the escape list. A long shot. We got slots which, unfortunately, never materialized.

One immediate requirement for sensible forgery was a sight of the original document and that was difficult. From our very early days as kriegies we had acquired the habit of 'finding' anything which looked useful. This could be achieved in many ways. One way was to pick the pockets of any workman who was required to do anything in camp. He would be working under guard himself, which brought the deed of acquiring down to a fine art. Suffice it to say that many's the tool and, not infrequently, the document which came our way. There were many ruses employed to further our aims, including blackmail. There would be, for instance, the occasional friendly goon who, during his routine of inspecting a block, would be engaged in conversation by the more fluent German-speakers among us. After a while he might be offered a cigarette and, having smoked it in the seclusion of one of our rooms, would go on his way rejoicing. By means of a little patience this performance would be repeated a few days later. Chocolate could also be used in this way. Having got his confidence and discovered how best he could help us, the question would be put. We only wanted to borrow things! But some things were more difficult than others; typing took a lot of persuasion, as did photographs for identity cards. There was one classic event when the Germans had us on the parade ground for identity checking and for fingerprinting. They had set up a table with their files, etc., and each of us in turn had to be checked and fingerprinted. Initially this all went well for them but having once 'been done', the officer in charge gave us to understand that we were more or less free to wander about. And since everything was going according to plan he decided to leave the corporal in charge. About half-way through this procedure the football, which had appeared and with which we had been fooling about, somehow found its way to the tables on which rested the Germans' paraphernalia! Naturally we did our best to help. We cursed those who had kicked the football, of course, and helped to pick up all those cards which had become so mixed up. We'd even salvaged the camera which, in a trice, was whisked away to photograph a potential escapee. So far so good. But we needed the printed photograph so we had to do a little barter, something on the lines of a roll of film and the use of the camera on some future occasion together with the required prints in exchange for the returned camera. That was a very reasonable exchange we thought. So, apart from the forgery itself, a lot of other skills were brought into play! The Germans, if caught helping us, stood a very good chance of being posted to the Eastern Front, a fact we had often to remind them of.

Roger was a 'natural' for Dean and Dawson since his ambition was to become an architect. When I told him about my 'hobby' he gladly joined. He had an extremely neat and steady hand and was probably the best of us all. Now we were five: Bushy Shore was the boss (he was in a bank before the war), then came Claud, previously a salesman, Pritchard, myself and now Roger. Quite a merry team who were taken care of by a number of 'stooges' who did the watch-keeping for us. We worked whenever the situation would allow, having taken precautions against a surprise intrusion by having a 'choir' on hand or a play rehearsal group ready to spring into action. The penalty for our pastime was the same as for 'incompetently approaching a German woman' . . . shooting!

Our work was, in the main, copying whatever documents we could get hold of, which, as explained earlier, was with some difficulty. In addition it was necessary to improvise, as in the case of letters. If a potential escapee was supposed to be travelling on business he would need letters of introduction and copies of correspondence to back up his story should he be challenged. This was the case with the documents for Ollie Philpot, who, with Codner and Williams, escaped using the 'Wooden Horse'. Ollie was a pilot on a sister squadron to myself. He knew I was a member of Dean and Dawson, so one day he called on me to see if I'd like to do a circuit. And so we set off to pound the circuit, as the expression had it. Soon he had explained his plan and his need for papers. He, in company with Codner and Williams, had a plan which was to build a vaulting horse on which everyone would be encouraged to exercise. This horse was to be placed outside the canteen about a third of the way between it and the perimeter wire and within full view of the goon-box. After it had been established for a short while the plan would begin in earnest. One or two people would be carried out within the box and, while others were 'exercising' over it, the chaps underneath would begin work. First, they had to construct a trap through which to enter the tunnel they would subsequently dig. The sand from the excavation would be loaded into little sacks and hung along the walls of the horse so that when the time came for *Appell* the workers and the sand could be carried back to the canteen. This required four strong men who should show no sign of strain as they lifted this whole contraption and its occupants from its place on the sand back into the canteen. The sand it contained had then to be distributed. There were various ways of doing this. It could be carried surreptitiously by visitors to the canteen and distributed gently over the 'playing field'. This required care since the new sand was totally different in colour from the normal surface sand. It could also be hidden above the ceiling in another block and in other ways. Anyway that was Ollie's plan. He went on to say that he would be travelling as a sales representative and as such would need letters of introduction, visiting cards, etc., and could I do them for him? He would, of course, need other documents such as an Identity Card, and a permit to travel, which everyone required. Of course I could not hope to produce all these myself, but I had time to do many, and so the plan was put to the others and work started in order to discover precisely what was required. It just so happened that by good fortune I had recently received a stick of Chinese Ink in a parcel from home. This was ideal for making a good density ink. Pens we had, but paper had to be of the right quality to simulate normal letter paper, a stiffer paper for the visiting cards, etc. I have no idea how many man-hours the task took for it was very demanding and errors would often require beginning again. We got some typing done through 'the good offices' of one of our tame goons, which was fortunate, for simulating typing was an awfully tedious business – but we managed. Such things as Identity Cards and the like posed less of a problem because they would naturally be part-worn through daily use. I then came to the letter headings. These obviously had to be something professional and so embossing was necessary. This was done with the head of a pin pressed carefully against the back of the lettering in the heading of the letter. Visiting cards too needed extra care; they shouldn't be too part-worn! The days and the weeks went by. While we were beavering away at our lettering the teams outside were getting fit leaping over the horse and the tunnellers beneath were working strenuously. Their work was so hard that from time to time they had to have a day off in order to recuperate. It was during one of these days that some idiot pushed the horse over as he failed to make the jump. Good team-work prevailed and the status quo was quickly restored. From then on it became common practice, very occasionally, to repeat that performance so that any spying goon could see for himself that it was perfectly harmless exercise we were engaged upon!

The long and the short of all this is that Michael Codner and Eric Williams, travelling together, arrived home safely and, shortly afterwards Ollie, who travelled quite on his own, reached home too. The next time I met Ollie Philpot was at a Royal British Legion meeting at which he was the speaker for that evening. I did not arrive in time to meet him before the talk began but I snuck in to hear what he had to say. I was really flattered to hear him say that, "a chap called Red Hunter had made some of his papers, and very useful they were".

Whilst at Warburg I had begun to think semi-seriously about my future when the war came to an end. My first choice would be to remain in the RAF but I tended to dismiss this mainly on the grounds that there would not be too many vacancies for Navigators and, in any case, competition would, doubtless, be pretty steep. It would be worth a try though. My second string would be a degree in Mechanical Engineering. It began at Warburg when I and a Fleet Air Arm Lieutenant, Squire Clayton, a Swordfish Navigator, started to work methodically through Gaunt's *Introduction to the Infinitesimal Calculus*. That was no mean 'introduction', which we nevertheless completed, albeit through a smoke haze, for Squire smoked a pipe and I cigarettes. Also in our room at the time was a Peter Bressey who was flying with Imperial Airways before the war but joined the RAF only to be shot down in the very early days. He taught me a great deal of navigation, especially astro-navigation. With this I figured I'd be able to take the First Class Navigators' exam when I got home. In any event these, together with my work in the 'travel agency' and tin-bashing kept me very busy indeed and, since it was quite demanding, I had little time in which to think of other things.

These activities were continued at Sagan where we were rather more fortunate in that we could obtain proper books for our studies. By dint of the generosity of the New Bodleian Library and the Red Cross, I got books on such things as physics and mechanics. With these, shared with others in exchange for books they'd been able to organize, one could study to some purpose. My first priority was to read for a B.Sc. Mech. Eng. In fact I was able to sit the First Year exam and, since the papers actually arrived home, I was encouraged to take the Intermediate exam a little later. It just so happened, however, that we had to move camp again and I had only one paper to write. That put paid to studies from then on as a kriegie.

Even from my early days I had a yen to make things. I've mentioned capacitors; the more commonplace things like mugs with handles, pans and chip-heaters (a little device consisting of a tin can within a tin can which could burn small fragments of coal from a cinder path with which to heat enough water for a brew) could all be made from the tins in which the Red Cross sent food in food parcels. But my *pièces de résistance* were steam engines. I built two: the first was a single-acting affair which at best did 670 rpm. Then I built a double-acting engine. This was intended to drive a boat, built by Tony Ingram, across the fire hydrant pond which was only three or four yards across but quite deep and naturally verboten to ourselves. The engine was a magnificent affair, with a water tube boiler fired by a fat lamp. Had we been able to salvage it I'm sure it would have been a great success! As it was, it blew up and found its way smartly to the bottom of the pond. It nearly came to grief sometime before all that, during its embryo stage in fact. It was the day of the landing in France. We had heard on 'Jimmy' that the invasion was on but when it was confirmed by the German radio by "*Das Oberkommando der Wehrmacht gibt bekannt . . .* that an attempted landing was driven back with heavy losses to the enemy," there was great rejoicing! And since I was in the process of building my monster, my first reaction was to throw the whole lot out of the window. I soon retrieved it all, however,

99

realizing that I might still have time to complete the project.

Tin-bashing equipment consisted first of all of an appropriate tin and silver paper from cigarette packets. The Red Cross always managed to send cigarettes with tin-foil, which, if collected and compacted and afterwards heated in a suitable tin and poured into a wooden mould, would make excellent solder. Then one requires a source of heat. This was provided by heating the German 'margarine' to extract the water and, with the aid of a wick made from something like a pyjama cord suspended in it, a fairly constant flame could be made. Then, by blowing into a blowpipe projecting into the flame, a hot, controllable flame could be obtained for soldering.

Alcohol played no great part in the life of a kriegie and I don't think it worried anyone that much. Nevertheless, when the opportunity presented itself certain people became quite adept at making it. Even at Warburg the enthusiasts managed to concoct a brew of kinds; at Sagan the art was brought to near perfection when we received what we termed 'bulk issue', a supply of dried fruit which originated from, I believe, the British Ambassador to Turkey, a Knatchbull Hugessen as I remember. We would pool our resources, put them into a bucket and add yeast tablets and the whole lot would ferment. Whilst at Warburg this fermenting mass, strained through a piece of cloth would suffice as a 'brew'. Here we were in the realms of sophistication which now required the specialist knowledge, in our block, of one Simpson to produce the final article. To his specification we built a condenser (the kind of thing we knew at school as a Liebig condenser) which consisted of a tube from the fire extinguisher connected to a series of cans surrounded by another series of cans through which ran cold water. This was placed on a larger can in which the mother liquor was gently boiled. The distillate was the real stuff. There was, however, a cut-off point beyond which one should not go. Boiling the whole thing to its end produced 'wood alcohol', which was not to be recommended. Before that stage the distillate was poured into bottles (supplied by the Germans and containing metal polish for which we paid *Lager Geld* or camp 'money') and, when stoppered, were buried in the sand outside the block for security. We chose bottles, rare though they were, in preference to tins for we feared that this mixture might penetrate the can before we would be able to drink it! If one were unfortunate enough to drink the last dregs of the distilled liquor it could, and did, have disastrous consequences. Bob Chadwick, who lived in the bunk above mine, had the unfortunate experience to drink some of this. Shortly after going to bed he decided to get up and get out of the window (we were always locked in at dusk) and walk to the wire. There he started to climb over. By dint of great good fortune the guard who saw him did not shoot. Instead he called the guardroom from which, in no time at all, a bevy of guards arrived to take him away. He was taken to the German sick quarters, via the cooler, from which he never again emerged into the camp. The happy part of that story is that he was eventually repatriated. It was several years before I again saw Bob. He visited GCHQ for briefing before going to the Far East and I gave him part of that briefing. That night he stayed with us in our cottage in Greet. I never saw him again. My wife and I had been on holiday in Switzerland; as we entered the aeroplane to return home we were given a newspaper in the normal way. The headlines of that paper announced that a British Officer had been lost overboard from a ship travelling to the Far East. It was Bob Chadwick. The reason for this was never discovered.

In every camp we took a fair amount of exercise quite voluntarily. It consisted for the most part of walking round and round the camp, known as doing a circuit. The usual call was 'Anyone for a circuit?' and one was never lost for a companion. We would walk round and round just chatting – after all the view was no great shakes, just pine trees and wire. There were many other forms of exercise available according to taste. Softball, the Canadian game, was very popular in the summer and the Canadian Red Cross provided the kit. We, under guidance from the Canadians, learned the game pretty well and organized leagues. Cricket, on the other hand, never did take off – only the British seemed to know the rules – and there was precious little in the way of equipment. Golf became very popular. The course was flat and all sand and, because we had no kit, we had to manufacture our own. Laying out a course was no problem; the greens were simply smoothed-out sand. Since there was no pro or shop available, ways and means had to be found to construct clubs and balls. Golf was one of those sports which required certain equipment which was not available in its true sense. The ball, for instance, was made from a marble core wound round many times, as regularly as possible, with thread, wool and the like to the standard size and then covered with a skin of leather from an old boot, cut 'tennis-ball-fashion' and sewn together with the strongest thread one could muster. Clubs were usually made from melted-down water jugs and poured into a sand mould ready to be assembled onto a stick which was made from the ubiquitious bedboard.

It was not long before word reached home of 'the golf course' we had at Sagan either through letters or via the Red Cross. So it was not long before some unfortunate kriegie would receive a letter from his wife saying something to the effect that she was so pleased to hear he was able to play golf again and had, accordingly, given his clubs to some poor German PoW who was working nearby! Rather like another piece of mis-information to reach home – our swimming pool. Again, I imagine the sources must have been the same. But this 'pool' I spoke of earlier was the fire hydrant pool, three or so yards square but deep. Alongside this was a large notice saying '*Kein Trinkwasser*', '*Baden ist verboten*'. The only time I ever heard of anyone bathing in it was almost a disaster. For some reason or other a kriegie was thrown in; it was a pretty warm day anyway, but the almost unfortunate part of it was that he couldn't get out. The sloping brick surround gave him nothing onto which to hold. Someone, however, did take pity on him eventually and gave him a helping hand.

Letters from home, infrequent as they were for many of us, quite often proved a source of great merriment. The custom was when anyone had any mail he would take it off to his bunk to read. Anything of outstanding interest which might have escaped the keen eyes of the censors was given a full airing. But when something humorous cropped up it was not unusual for the reader to leap up in his bunk and announce to the room, "Listen to this". There were such snippets as "Mother was right, and I've decided to marry Harry. You remember? That nice chap who used to beat you at golf". Or someone's girlfriend would write, "I hope you're having as much fun as I am". Another, "I've met such a nice young Army officer". One rather cruel remark was, "How lucky I was not to have married a cowardly prisoner of war". "Do the guards teach you German?" caused some amusement too. Sometimes we'd receive photographs which we'd pin to the wall by our bunks. One surprising incident occurred when, by chance, one chap visited another for a chat and happened to notice a picture of a nice-looking girl stuck to the wall saying, "She's just like my wife". It turned out that it was (or had been) his wife, who, because he'd been in the bag for so long and she hadn't heard from him, decided to marry another. I think the two chaps became great friends.

I've mentioned 'new purges', the arrival of new kriegies. On one purge we had one particularly gormless character who arrived in our room. He was distinctly odd and quite oblivious to having his leg pulled. We thought he looked a bit like a horse so, naturally, we christened him Harry the Horse. He wanted to know what things were like, etc. and we explained that things were tough at times. In fact they had been so bad one kriegie had died, but we didn't tell the Germans so that we could draw his rations. In the cupboard there was a skeleton to prove it! The skeleton belonged to Bill Kerr who was an early kriegie and had been allowed to purchase it to further his studies! Another trick we thought quite clever at the time was our tame bird. We would watch this imaginary bird fly around the room and alight on a stool or something. We became very adept at following this bird around, all turning our heads at the same time. And Harry thought *we* were crazy.

Life went by without too many tragedies, such as the loss of tunnels or equipment, for some time. But on 24 March 1944 we had a serious jolt. The German Commandant came to the camp with a large number of guards. He went straight to the room of the SBO Group Captain Dickie Kellett, while the guards shouted to us to go outside for *Appell*. When we'd assembled in our usual dishevelled manner the German officer and the SBO came on the scene. This was a most unusual event and could only bode ill. And sure enough it did. The SBO had to tell us that fifty British officers had been shot "attempting to escape". A number of them I knew personally. The escape had been from one of the three large tunnels Tom, Dick and Harry dug from the North camp. The escape had taken place from Harry some days before and it had upset the Germans a great deal. In fact, as we learned later, it had caused great consternation throughout Germany. Even the Gestapo had been involved (Himmler had long since tried to get control of Allied PoWs but had so far been resisted by Goering) and it was they who had shot our colleagues "whilst resisting arrest". The Commandant himself was almost in tears; he knew as we did that it was a prisoner's duty to attempt to escape, that we were unarmed and should be treated in accordance with the Geneva Convention. The Commandant, although hard-pressed at times by our antics, remained an officer and gentleman. It was his 'leniency' which caused him to be 'relieved' of his appointment. We never saw him again. We were then resolved to do our utmost to let the goons see and know how much we hated them.

Escapes were, for the time being, forbidden but that didn't stop tunnels being dug in great profusion and papers being made. They would always come in handy! There was, naturally, a great deal of sand generated by all the work which was going on and a home had to be found for it. Accordingly, new means had to be found. One ingenious method was the construction of a large number of little bags which would be carried beneath the voluminous Polish greatcoats which were all the rage. As many people as possible collected a bag and, when summoned to *Appell*, we would wander every which way around the camp shedding a little at a time onto the duller-coloured sand on the surface. Another way was to hide as much as possible in the roof area of a selected hut. This proved quite hilarious when on one occasion the chosen ceiling decided enough was enough. It happened a short while before an *Appell*, almost at the time the goons were making their accustomed way through the huts shouting at us to get outside. The goon who witnessed this shambles wasted no time in making his discovery known and all hell was let loose! We spent much of that day outside whilst they tried to find the source. Sources there were aplenty!

Tunnels always required to be shored to prevent the sand from caving in and this was done with bedboards. It wasn't long before there was hardly a bedboard to be had and a means had to be found to replace them. The solution lay in the string from parcels which, up till then, had been discarded in the parcels compound, or that which we considered superfluous to our other requirements! It now became a serious commodity and even the smallest pieces were salvaged and made into pieces long enough to be wound under and over from side to side of the bunks. In fact this made a much more comfortable bunk than the bedboards it replaced.

6

On the Move

In the winter of 1944/5 rumours of yet another move were prevalent. A tame goon had whispered that something was about to take place, although he couldn't say precisely when. This news confirmed our suspicion that because of the Russian advances, we would most likely be moved on. After all, there were by this time some 10,000 Air Force prisoners of one kind and another in this huge complex of camps, most of whom no doubt were Americans. It was unlikely the Germans would want them to fall into the hands of the Allies. There was another rumour, not quite so pleasing perhaps, that we were to be held hostage. Whenever and wherever made no difference and we began making prudent provision. Most had accumulated some small reserves against the possibility of harder times, including a few briquettes of coal. We had no intention of leaving behind anything which would be of use. First requirements, however, were the construction of the means of carrying our gear. I still had my original battledress trousers which, when sewn and tied up, made a presentable haversack. Roger Simmons, Ron Simmich (a New Zealander) and myself decided (it was not so much of a decision as a natural event) to travel together and although many others decided to construct sledges on which to haul their gear we reasoned that should a sledge break down en route it would be a problem to transfer what we had to an alternative means of transport. We decided, therefore, to carry all we could, although we did succumb later on. One thing was certain: we would need to wear as much warm clothing as possible for it was mid-winter and winters in Germany could be, and were, very cold. As a 'tin-basher' I immediately set to work to make water bottles and other accessories for the journey. Meanwhile, 'Jimmy' kept us informed of events regarding the Allies' movements and the war's progress and our spirits were high.

Finally the suspense was over and we were told that we had to be ready to move at 11.30 that night, 27 January. I rolled all my drawings and tied them with string from my bed and placed them in my 'locker' with my remaining books with a label addressed to me in England! Who was going to find and forward them didn't concern me. It was just an idea. My notes, however, should not be left behind since I'd spent so much time writing them. My diary too; from quite early in the bag I'd managed to keep a diary of sorts on scraps of paper which I concealed in a hollow made in a bedpost. There was nothing of any great merit noted in it, almost entirely personal jottings. I also had a small sketch book in which I'd made drawings of the rooms and some of the equipment we made. Roger wrote in his exceedingly neat hand a verse of a poem, 'Not by Eastern windows only' to celebrate my entering my fourth year as a kriegie. Such things I'd certainly not leave behind!

John Lloyd, Bill Roe and Roger began making oatcakes, which they cooked to a golden brown on our overheating stove. Coffee was available and the food reserves which we couldn't subdivide easily were issued by Frank Reade as evenly as he could. I inherited a tin of jam! With the aid of a spoon I demolished it in record time. I had achieved one of my kriegie ambitions! Time wore on as one postponement followed another until at 6 on the morning of the 28th we finally moved off as a body. There were nearly a thousand of us. We collected a Red Cross parcel apiece on our way out and finally departed into the unknown at 0800 hrs.

The SBO had ruled that no attempt at escape should be made during the march out of Sagan; for one thing the weather was definitely against us. Many of the guards escorting us appeared to have been imported specially for the occasion and were, by and large, older than we had seen around during life inside the wire. Presumably the younger, fitter types had been despached to one of the fronts. Those marching alongside us were finding this no joke as they tried to keep us in some sort of column. Their rations were little better than ours and consisted of the oats-cum-sawdust-type bread and a can of meat paste. For them not only the present but also the future must have looked pretty grim.

The events of the next few days are recorded on odd scraps of paper which once, in part, constituted my diary. During the early part of the march, I decided there would be little future in carting or dragging through the snow any superfluous kit. I wouldn't be able to eat it! So I threw out some books and one or two pieces of 'junk', including the little roll of paper, my diary. It was one of my least rational moves. I must have been in a state of mental aberration. From the few remaining sheets, written around the time of the march I can quote.

Saturday 27 January 1945.   "Wrote the second part of the Engineering Drawing paper for Inter B.Sc. (Mech. Eng). Jerry Pitt and I were the only two stayers, the rest have thrown in on account of the news and rumours.

"This evening I got stuck into making water bottles for the chaps in the room – soldering lids and handles onto Klim and other tins. I'd made only four when the panic started. We were told to be ready to move off at 11.30 pm. I had my pack nearly ready and so spent time sewing and pinning things together. That which grieved me most was not the thought of a forced march to anywhere but the thought of leaving my sole worldly possessions of the last three and a half years, my mail, photos, books and all my drawings and reserve clothing, and the fact that I had only one more paper to write for my Inter exam. And I don't think I lie when I say I think I was doing pretty well.

"Sentiment apart, we have to move and that right soon. We put briquettes which we had been saving for a rainy day in the stove and got a really solid coffee brew going and had the odd quick bash (eating more than usual) through the 'generosity' of our room quartermaster, Frank Reade. My allocation was a tin of jam which enabled me to achieve one of my kriegie ambitions of bashing a tin of jam with a spoon! Time wore on. The move was postponed an hour at the time. We decided to employ the time by using some flour and making some shortbread. This was started by John Lloyd and continued by Bill Roe and Roger Simmons."

Sunday 28th. "At about 0600 we prepared to move and finally moved as a body of about 1,000 from East Camp. We collected a Red Cross parcel apiece on our way out and finally left camp at 0800.

"The first town we passed was Helmsdorf and after 14 km we stopped in a most barren spot for 'lunch' for 30 minutes. There was no mean wind blowing and a fair amount of hard snow. Arrived Haldau about 1600 hours – 18 km – where we got some hot water, and some of us hot Reich coffee from civilians who, for the most part, seemed sympathetic.

"For about two hours we hung around the town square hoping to get some place to sleep. During this time we bought two very ropey sledges from the locals for forty cigarettes. Then our camp was split into two parties, one to be billetted in a church and the other in a school. Roger, Ron and I plumped for the lower ground floor of the school – concrete – and got a small space. The only way to keep warm was to sleep eight deep. In fact, that was all space would permit. No food or hot water were provided and the temperature in the night was down to minus 18 Centigrade; during the march minus 10 Centigrade. (If nothing else we always came across thermometers – perhaps to let us know just how miserable we should be!)"

Monday 29th. "Spent the day at Haldau to let the Americans from Belaria and North Camp get ahead again. Roger traded a tin of bully for a loaf of bread – otherwise no rations. One *Appell* in half a blizzard and told tomorrow's trek would be 25 km."

Tuesday 30th. "Left at 0100 hours dragging everything we had on our sledges etc., destination Priebus. Evacuees on the road hindered our progress no end. Arrived Lieppa, distance 11 km, at 1600 hours. Here we were billeted in a school. No lights and still no food. We lit a fire for hot water and afterwards retired to bed in the attic which was literally knee-deep in kriegies. Still damned cold but only minus 7 Centigrade in the night."

Wednesday 31st. "Set course Muskau at 16.10 hours. A very hard day – hardest yet. Lack of food quite noticeable – scarcely enough to keep us warm. Snow and wind were bad and the roads treacherous. The last five kilometers were very hard going as the thaw had set in and the sledges went deep into the snow. Upon our arrival at a glass factory in Muskau the French and other workers were most helpful and generous with hot water and often coffee. They were also most amenable to bargaining for bread. Oberfeldwebel Stuhlmeyer (previously NCO i/c guards at Luft 3 and a man who did his awkward duty quite fairly by the kriegies) managed to get us billeted in this glass factory, the manager of which had been a PoW in America in the last war and did everything he possibly could to help. SBO put us on parole as regards damage. The factory people gave us a free hand to the extent of providing coal for fires. We utilized the furnaces to the full extent for making hot water and drying clothes. I didn't sleep much at night for I was in an outhouse which filled with smoke which necessitated leaving the door open thereby making it pretty chilly."

Thursday lst February. "Spent day at Muskau during which time we carried out an inspection on the sledge; didn't favour putting on such wheels as we could find or manufacture. Maggie Roth set the pace by standing at the factory gate with a tin of coffee and a D-bar shouting at the passing civilians, *"Kaffee und Schokolade für alten Kinderwagen"* and, what's more, he got one. Others turned out wooden wheels in the lathe

110

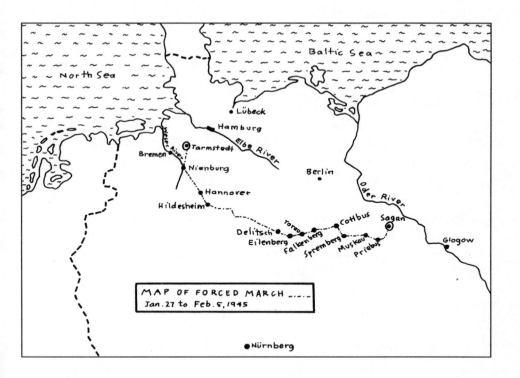

MAP OF FORCED MARCH
Jan. 27 to Feb. 5, 1945

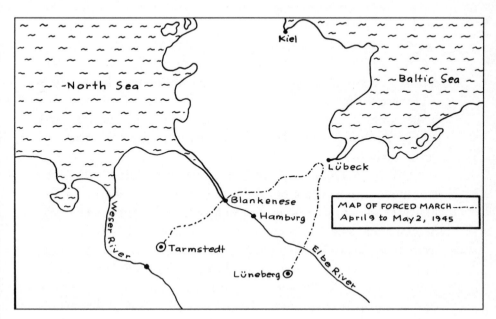

MAP OF FORCED MARCH
April 9 to May 2, 1945

111

shop. Although the thaw seems to have set in we still intend to take our sledge, lightly laden, and our packs on our backs. Received half a loaf of bread per man and marching orders for 21.30 hours. This was later changed to 22.30 hours, at which time we left. The air raid which we hoped would prevent our move tonight, and the extreme darkness, seemed to have no bearing on the matter – we left. The East Camp was split into blocks 62 (ours), 63, 64 , 66 and 67, and the rest. They would leave tomorrow for Nürnberg – possibly.

Friday 2nd.   "Marched through the night. We jettisoned our sledge after about seven km but carried all our gear. What a shambles. Bods lying in ditches, packs and belongings lying around them. We (Roger, Ron and I) kept going pretty well but were fairly teased out soon after dawn. Eventually arrived at a village, Graustein, near which we, and most everyone else, spied some milk in churns outside a farm and we wasted no time in transferring the contents to ourselves.

"Just outside this village we were directed towards a large barn. This barn was the best thing yet, packs were hurled into the hay and we just dived in on top. We didn't stir till two hours later to continue our trek to Spremburg, a further eight km. Arrived at 15.15 hours. We were set down in some *panzer-schule* and were issued with a fair amount of brattling soup – and were promised some water later. We left before we could avail ourselves of the water and marched to the goods yard where we hung around till after dark waiting to entrain in cattle wagons.

"During our wait we noticed a scruffy-looking individual coming along the track beside the wagons in a very nonchalant manner, sometimes whistling to himself, as he opened the axle box of each wheel in turn and from time to time would pour in oil from a can. He also added something from a bag hanging inside his coat. He was quietly adding a little sand to the lubricant – for luck! Being escorted by a guard meant that conversation was limited. Nevertheless, he said, "When you get to Blighty tell 'em we're coming too". And he went on his way rejoicing – a typical British Tommy. He did my heart a power of good, and probably others too.

"We finally boarded, 43 in our wagon and they were only designed to take '40 *hommes ou 8 chevaux (en long)*'. Expecting to spend the night in this siding we got weaving making a fire to boil our brew can. We were doing very well until it was decided we should leave at 23.30 hours. In the ensuing panic to collect our gear once more John Lloyd knocked the hot water over. That was the nearest we've been to having a hot brew for some time. The only thing left to do was to try to bed down somehow. I spent the night on top of some blokes. We were fortunate in being issued with a Red Cross parcel before we left the siding. Where those parcels came from I do not know but they could hardly have come at a more opportune moment."

Saturday 3rd. "Spent the day on the train – pretty chilly but derived a certain amount of rest although we all ached through being unable to move. Passed through Hannover."

Sunday 4th. "Arrived Tarmstedt Ost at 16.30 hrs and marched to a camp 4 km away. Now we come to the bitter bit; we waited outside the camp gates, wallowing in mud and in drizzling rain until 01.30 hours – the worst part of the whole journey. Damned cold and tired and no choice but to walk around in very restricting circles in order to keep warm. When we were let in we were given a very cursory search and directed to some derelict barracks where, with the greatest of ease, we parked on the floor till 10.30 next morning."

Monday 5th. "Moved to permanent quarters, block 22 room 3, which has a most teased-out stove, no lights, no beds, practically nothing. We stopped-up holes in the floor, dismantled and tried to re-assemble the stove."
This was Marlag und Milag Nord, Tarmstedt.

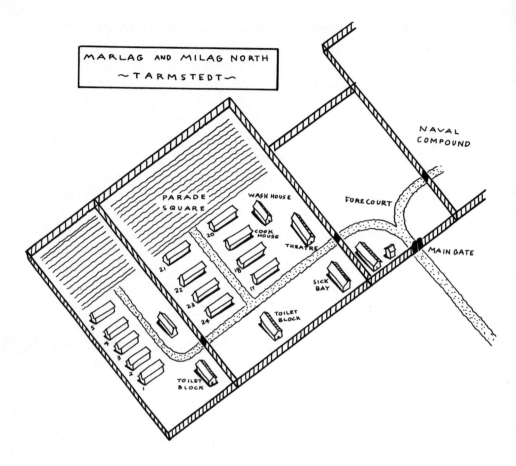

Our days in camp were now numbered, certainly in smaller numbers than hitherto. Spring could not be far off and the end must be in sight. We spent our time making-do and mending; there was precious little to scrounge but we managed to find oddments around the place with which to furnish our abode – sparsely. The few remaining impressions of this desert of a place are the poor food and the lack of organization. Our rations consisted of a black treacly type of bread which, surprisingly, we found to be quite nourishing, and a sausage paste. We got to like these as time went by, even though this diet lacked variety; they were said to be submariners' rations. The disorganization mani-fested itself in irregular *Appells* and a complete lack of

114

information concerning our future, for we were sure it could 'not be long now'.

In due course we were on the road once more. Our destination was said to be Lübeck. It was now some three years since I'd been 'stationed' there and memories of it were far from favourable.

It was spring (when a young man's fancy is said to turn to thought of something or other – I'll try to remember!) and the outlook was decidedly brighter. At this time we hadn't much gear to transport, just the bare essentials. Accordingly we moved off into the countryside and were going one knew not where. The weather was warmer and the countryside did indeed look inviting! Somewhere along the road we drew level with a field of rhubarb (not very ripe as I recall.) Now, an opportunity such as that was not to be ignored and the whole column simply diverted, guards or no guards, through this field and cut a very neat swathe through it. For some considerable distance along the road thereafter we left a fine trail of rhubarb leaves. The aftereffects of that foray were not quite so happy for some, for, not to put too fine a point on it, it proved to be something of a laxative.

It was during this journey that our syndicate acquired a pram. We came to a halt in the village square; the village name escapes me. The point was we needed transport and sure enough in this village there appeared before us several opportunities. There were women pushing prams. In our best kriegie German we started to ask first one then another whether they would be prepared to sell their pram for chocolate or coffee. And we bought our pram, not a large or ostentatious machine you understand; a simple green affair with four good wheels. The lady concerned was delighted as she lifted junior out and grabbed the flimsy blanket, etc., and took our coffee and a 'D-Bar' of chocolate. We were happy too for we could simply put our packs into this and it virtually ran itself from there on.

Another opportunity to put our new transport to the test came very soon afterwards. Ron bartered for some potatoes and later we got some onions for a few cigarettes. We could have a stew that night! During the first part of our march we were delivered into a field where it soon became evident we would be staying a while, so without too much ado we began making preparations for a place to sleep. This was accomplished by digging an area and piling the turves so removed on what we estimated to be the windward side of the ditch, the idea being to sleep in the hole and to cover ourselves with the ubiquitous Polish greatcoat. Nearby we found a supply of straw in bales. This was indeed a boon and we set out to gather enough to sleep on. During my foray I almost came to grief at the hands of the Hitler Jugend, young boys and girls dressed in a kind of scout uniform. I was feeling very pleased with myself for having found a bale before they all disappeared and was making my way back when there was a boyish shout from behind me. I nonchalantly turned around only to find one of these creatures shouting and pointing a rifle at me. A couple of prods from his rifle gave me the impression he didn't like what I was doing. He was ordering me to return the bale, so I dumped it on the ground. Apparently that was not the idea at all for he waved his rifle in all directions and shouted some more before pointing to where I'd been. I had to admit defeat and picked up the bale and, under escort, took it back. Roger had more luck and brought back enough straw to line the pit we'd dug. Meanwhile Ron had got some water and was busy trying to get a small fire to burn in order to make a brew. Then followed the height of contentment, sitting in a field, beside a fire and a brew of coffee with my friends.

From there we set off next morning heading towards Lübeck which was still some way off. Somehow we got to hear that there was an outbreak of cholera. True or not, the SBO remonstrated with the Germans, telling them that the war was nearly over and it would be in no one's interest to go much further. As a result we were directed towards a farm. The party was split, one going round a lake to some barns on the far side, whereas we were herded into a large barn nearby. This was a monument of a barn which had a ladder inside leading into a hay loft. Again, tired and weary, we clambered up this ladder and threw ourselves into the hay and fell sound asleep for some time. By now the guards were sadly depleted and those in evidence could not have cared less. They were far from home with little hope of improving their miserable lot. They'd lost, as we always told them they would. Now we roamed freely. Some enterprising types had made a sign which they pinned to a tree along the lane. The sign read: "Good pull-in for tanks" with an arrow pointing towards our 'estate'. At about 10.00 next morning, sure enough, along came a couple of scout cars. In no time at all they were issuing copies of the *Daily Mirror* and white bread. This bread was like cake to us who'd eaten only the German bread for so long. But food was of secondary importance now for we were FREE.

Recollections of what followed, although of no major significance otherwise, were of pure unadulterated joy.

Roger, Ron and I decided it would be rather pleasant if we could find a car and drive home. In a little while we found a car, a staff car and a Mercedes to boot. Fuel there was by the hundreds of gallons in the centre of the autobahn, so we borrowed a few cans, filled the car and loaded the seats with more and then parked it in a nearby wood. Next day would see us homeward bound. We would simply head westwards, hit the coast, drive to the nearest port and then scrounge a lift on one of the many ships that would certainly be there. From then on it would be merry England all the way. It was going to be the best outing one could ever plan. Next morning, however, there was little more than a track, from where our limousine had been parked, leading to the road. Hell's bells! Some miserable sod had pinched it.

Then came the message that we were to be ready to move off again. This time we were going under our own steam, so to speak, by command of the SBO, to an airfield on Lüneberg Heath from where we hoped we'd be flown home, courtesy of the RAF.

And that was how it worked out. The wait wasn't long (and this time we didn't mind waiting for a while). In due course a Lanc appeared and was quickly taxied back down the runway and as many as could leapt aboard. We couldn't make the first one but got on the next. This was from 460 Squadron flown by Aussies

and, I think, based at Binbrook in Lincolnshire. The accommodation was, if anything, more cramped than the cattle wagons of
times already long since passed. But who cared? The skipper
wasn't worried so why should anyone else? We certainly enjoyed
every minute of the short flight home. I was somewhere in the
nose so I had a wonderful view as the sun shone down on
England's green and pleasant land. The fields had never been
greener or more welcoming than now. At Dunsfold we were
welcomed by the beautiful young ladies of PMRAFNS (Princess
Mary's Royal Air Force Nursing Service) and the QARANC
(Queen Alexandra's Royal Army Nursing Corps) who served us
with food and drink (squash) and seemed to make quite a fuss of
us, scruffy though we were. After an hour or so, we were detailed
off to lorries waiting to take us somewhere. It didn't matter
where, but, as it happened, we were driven up to London there to
entrain for Cosford. In London we were soon embroiled in a mass
of traffic and people milling around in all directions. We hadn't
expected such a welcome and, sure enough, it wasn't for us they
were waiting. It just so happened they were waiting for the 'great
man' himself. Winston Churchill was due to pass that way. By
strange chance we found ourselves driving along no more than a
couple of vehicles behind him. Although we weren't exactly
returning heroes we received a great welcome; well who was to
know?

Cosford was expecting us and, although the NCOs and airmen
weren't quite so good looking as the young ladies at Dunsfold,
they were efficient. They collected our 'rubbish' or as much as we
were prepared to part with, gave us forms to fill in (and there were
some peculiar answers on those forms), handed out clothes and
eventually gave us a travel warrant apiece to our home and
directed us to the lorries waiting to take us to the station. From
then on everything seemed quite normal again. That is until our
arrival home. In my case, as I came along the road to where I once
lived, there was a banner across the road: "Welcome Home Jim".
That really said it all for it was a welcome such as no other
welcome had ever been or ever could be.

118

7

Home

There was Mum, Dad, my sister Betty and Steve and, for some reason strange to me at the time, Renie. But there was no Don, my brother. I soon learned that he had been killed in the previous September near Arnhem on 'Operation Market Garden'. This was terrible. He was in a reserved occupation working on aircraft engines, both civil and military, with what was British Airways in South Wales. He need not have gone into the Army at all. But, as Mum told me, he joined the Welsh Guards to do his bit to get me home sooner. They had chosen not to tell me in their letters 'for fear of worrying me'.

It was so good to see everyone; they hadn't changed so much in close on four years despite all the hardships they had endured. I'm sure I did a lot of talking but I don't suppose anyone listened. It was just so good to be back home. My mother had prepared a feast suitable for a king, and all from their meagre rations. Everything was so sparkling clean and neat in contrast to what I'd become accustomed to for a while. As we spoke there were tears appearing in my mother's eyes and her voice was so soft. Father, on the other hand, hadn't too much to say but even his voice was a trifle uneven as he spoke. Steve was just Steve – no doubt he could recall his homecoming some years back, after the last war. Steve was the father of a very good friend of mine whilst we were still at school. Peter and I were the best of chums for several years until he died of polio at the age of 13, I think it was. This had devastated Steve's life. It had certainly been a sad blow to me. For some reason Steve had kind of adopted me, taken a great interest in my progress at school and later he helped me to get a job, first in a stockbroker's office and later in the Bank. I was so glad he was in the little welcoming party. Naturally, I was delighted to see Renie too. We'd been out of touch, apart from two letters I believe, since before the war. I then learned, however, that she was now married so that put a damper on any of those foolish ideas I'd quietly cherished whilst a kriegie. It did seem odd that she should have been there today except, as I learned later, my mother had told her I would be coming home. There was also another reason. Whilst at Luft 3, Roger and I were doing one of the many circuits one day when we began talking of the future and our ambitions. Roger was determined to become an architect, and, like me, he had studied whilst in the bag. He also confided that he would, all things being equal, marry Iris, his fiancée. Similarly, I told him I'd carry on with my studies to become a Mechanical Engineer, that was if I couldn't stay in the RAF, and I'd ask Renie to marry me. Such were the daydreams of a couple of blokes whilst pounding the circuit long ago. Unknown to me till Renie told me, Roger had used one of his three letters one month to write to Renie on my behalf. I think I'd written once or twice but because I'd no idea how long I'd be away I thought it unfair to expect her to wait for me. Roger's letter had reached its destination but, as it happened, it arrived either on the day before or on the day of her wedding to an Army chap with whom she was working in the Air Ministry. And that was why she had arranged to come to see me on my return.

Little did I know then that this was a blessing in disguise. For although it took some four years to show itself I was to be far more fortunate than I could ever have imagined. In 1947 I, by a strange and somewhat tortuous route, met Elsa. Had anyone told me that such a thing could happen I would almost certainly have considered the odds very long indeed. The long and the short of it is that we met and, some two years later, were married on 27 June 1949 to live happily ever after, at least to date, and I hope this arrangement will last for ever. This romance, however, must

1. The very first Beaufort, 1938. Probably at Martlesham Heath.

2. Uxbridge, 1940. The author is standing fourth from the left.

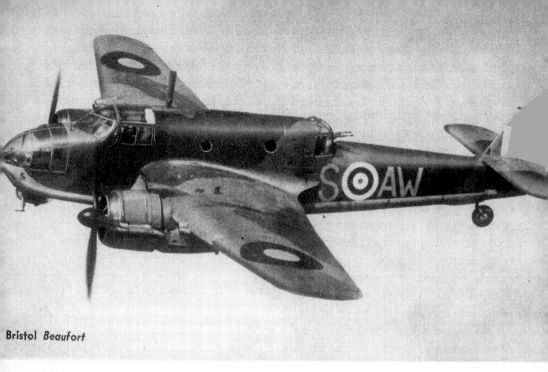

Bristol *Beaufort*

3. Official Air Ministry postcard.

4. Photograph of 217 Squadron Beaufort.

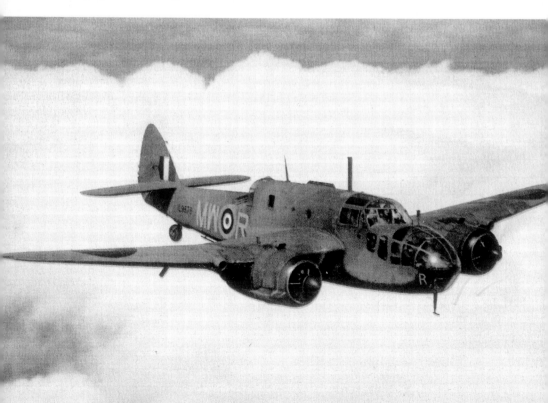

5. The *Scharnhorst* in 1939. Note the armoured belt around the stern.

6. Bombing Instruction Class, December, 1940. The author is second from the left.

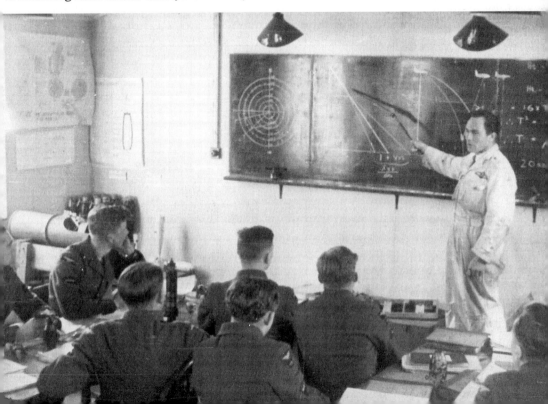

7. The author holding £180's worth of bombsight!

8. Bombing and Gunnery School, December, 1940. The author is the tallest in the back row. The aircraft is a Fairey Battle.

9. 217 Squadron, St Eval. *Left to right:* the author, Pilot Officer Gibson, Pilot Officer Tom Kitching DFC.

10. 217 Squadron Mess, Waterbeach Hotel. *From left:* Spencer Schrader, Leo Collings, Jack Gibson, Tom Kitchen, the author.

each Hotel – 217 Sqn Mess

cer Schrader
Collings
ck Gibson

11. No. 1 Dress, Oflag XXIB, Schubin, Poland; probably for the King's Birthday Parade. The author is in the centre at the back.

12. More usual Kriegie attire. *From left:* Chadwick, Hunter, Parsons, Paterson.

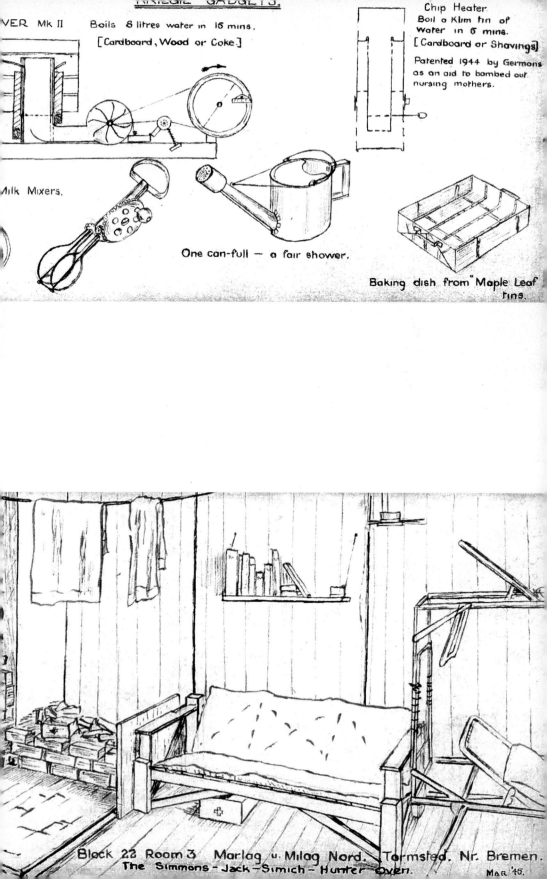

KRIEGIE GADGETS.

...VER Mk II   Boils 8 litres water in 15 mins.
[Cardboard, Wood or Coke.]

Chip Heater.
Boil a Klim tin of
Water in 6 mins.
[Cardboard or Shavings]
Patented 1944 by Germans
as an aid to bombed out
nursing mothers.

Milk Mixers.

One can-full — a fair shower.

Baking dish from "Maple Leaf"
tins.

Block 22 Room 3   Marlag u. Milag Nord.   Tarmsted. Nr. Bremen.
The Simmons - Jack - Simich - Hunter Oven.   MAR '45.

15. The Crazy Section. Arts and Crafts Exhibition, October 1943. Mousetrap; toast rack, a Bookie Bob production; steam engine.

16. The Winter March, 1945.

form a section on its own for such an event cannot be dismissed so summarily.

It would be totally unfair to end this little epistle without further reference to my parents and the hardships they endured in those years of the war. Betty, my sister, had lived at home but worked in London as a telephonist. Donald, my brother, had been evacuated at the outbreak of war to South Wales where British Airways moved, lock, stock and barrel. When I went home on leave there was hardly a night we didn't spend in the air raid shelter at the bottom of the garden. And there were daylight raids too. One night a bomb fell and landed under the house. Fortunately it didn't explode but whilst it was being dug out my mother and father had to move out of their home and stay with neighbours a way off. Then they had the anguish of not knowing for quite some time after being notified of my 'missing on operations' that I was still alive. Apparently, however, 'Lord Haw-Haw' of German radio propaganda fame, who was in the habit of announcing the names of any prisoners taken from all three services, was the first to confirm my being a PoW. Of course it was a ploy to encourage relatives and friends of people serving in the force to listen for such events (and of course the propaganda given out at the same time). The fact that he mentioned our crew at least shortened my parents' anguish by a couple of days. The Air Ministry was always most cautious about notifying parents, wives and relatives of casualties, which was understandable. They then had only the barest knowledge of my welfare during the years which followed. But the most crippling blow of all must surely have been the news of their second son, Donald, being killed in action on 27 September 1944. All this they bore with such courage and gave me a hero's welcome on my return into the bargain. There were times when I imagined I was hard done by but how much greater was their suffering and worry for which there were never any flags flown or bugles blown. They, like so many parents of their time, survived through plain guts, faith and perseverance. And I'd sat on my backside through all that.

As for my two stalwart colleagues in my darkest days, Roger

Simmons and Ron Simmich, Ron was killed in a flying accident in 1947 when he flew into a mountain after his return to New Zealand. Roger married Iris, became a most successful architect and had two sons and a daughter, but he died on 31 August 1975. He achieved so much in his lifetime, he had made and maintained friendships the world over and was sadly missed by all. No one could have had a greater friend than Roger, a totally selfless and sincere person. I had the sad but great honour to make the address at his funeral in Esher in September 1975.

After a few weeks' leave I was recalled to the RAF on an Extended Service Commission and began refresher flying training ostensibly in order to join 'Tiger Force' to fly against the Japs. Fortunately that theatre folded up before I was fit to join in. During the course of this, having previously applied for a Permanent Commission, I was invited to go to Sunningdale before a Permanent Commission selection board. Perhaps I treated this less seriously than I should for I actually enjoyed the tests, both physical and mental. There were several highly qualified gentlemen also doing the same thing but rather more seriously it seemed. Nevertheless I was offered a Permanent Commission as a Navigator. Strangely enough, on the same day I received notification from, I think it was, the New Bodleian at Oxford, that in view of my having taken the First Year exam for the B.Sc. Eng. course (which I'd taken at Sagan) I was eligible to continue study for which the university would be pleased to pay! This placed me in a position I'd never in my wildest dreams considered. I had no one to whom I could reasonably turn for advice (so I cannot put the blame on anyone else for my decision). I decided to accept the offer made me by the Air Ministry and returned to flying. What might have happened had I decided otherwise I have no means of knowing, although, from all accounts, there would have been plenty of openings for qualified mechanical engineers at the time I could have expected to qualify. My career in the RAF was hardly outstanding but I enjoyed what I did and, by and large, made the grade to retire at the compulsory retiring age of 55 having retained my General Duties status throughout.

I suppose I must be something of a fatalist at heart for without much intervention from me things worked out very well. Had I chosen to go to university I wonder whether I'd have met Elsa. Perhaps 'fate' would have taken a hand and arranged for us to meet by an even more devious route. I'm sure it would.

Appendix 1

Brief biographies of some of the author's fellow prisoners

LOU BARRY

Squadron Leader Louis (Lou) Barry was born in 1909 and grew up in Hungary, where his father, the noted rower W. A. Barry, taught him to scull and to ride on the estate on which he was employed. After World War I he became a professional sculler on the Thames, winning the Doggetts Coat and Badge in 1927, and gaining the championship of England in 1936, beating Ted Phelps. Later the same year he lost the championship when Ted's younger brother Eric beat him.

During this time he was also working as a professional rowing coach, first in Ireland and then in Italy, where in 1936 he coached the Italian Olympic team. It was there that he was given a medal by Mussolini. He used to joke that he just happened to be at the end of the welcoming line when Mussolini made a visit and since everyone was getting a medal there was no way of avoiding it.

When war broke out he joined the RAF, qualified as a navigator and air gunner and was shot down over Germany. He escaped twice but was both times recaptured. He remained a PoW for five and a half years.

One of the feats for which he will always be remembered was that he was a major figure in the distribution of BBC news received on clandestine radios in the camps in which he was imprisoned. This highly risky activity, for which the penalties were harsh, was one of the most carefully guarded secrets of PoW life. It involved the manufacture of radio sets, the concealment of them through frequent searches and movements from one camp to another and, finally, the spreading of the news in such a way as not to bring guards into the camp or alert suspicions. In fact this whole operation was so successful that there was hardly a day in Stalag Luft III when BBC news was not available. Even during the forced marches of spring 1945 the radio was in action. The contribution this made to PoW morale throughout the war was immense. Even when the news was not particularly good, it was a point of pride that the reports were getting through and it allowed the men to feel they were not powerless. After the war Barry was awarded the MBE for his efforts.

Following the close of hostilities Barry worked in Austria in Air Intelligence, where he remained until his retirement in 1965. He also continued to coach rowing – he became involved in the Tideway Scullers School – and he took the British crews to the Olympics in Tokyo in 1964, and to Montreal in 1976. At the time there was no official British National squad, nor was there any position of head coach, but Barry was generally acknowledged to be the expert on such matters. When he died, on 8 April 1991, he was the last surviving professional sculling champion of England. He was 82.

AIDAN CRAWLEY

Aidan Crawley led a life that reads like something out of an adventure novel. He was a brilliant cricketer (listed seven consecutive years in "Lord's Week", 1924 to 1930), a crusading journalist, a daring pilot, an intrepid escaper, a Labour party minister, a major force in television in both the BBC and ITN, then a Conservative MP after he left the Labour party in 1957. He remained an MP until 1967 when London Weekend Television appointed him chairman and he stepped down from his elected position. He eventually became president of the company.

He was born on 10 April 1908, and educated at Harrow and at Trinity College, Oxford. In 1928 he made a record total of 1,137 runs for Oxford, which included five centuries. He was expected to play for England (he was named as twelfth man on one occasion) but he was already leading a life that was too full to allow for regular sporting fixtures. He travelled to North Borneo for Unilever, and after a conversation with Esmond Harmsworth, the son of Viscount Rothermere, he began to work for the *Daily Mail* in 1930. When he arrived he was immediately sent to France to cover the R101 airship disaster.

While working for the *Daily Mail* he also kept up with his great love, hunting. He hunted with sixty-six different packs of hounds during this time. Yet he was not quite the establishment figure he might at first sight seem. While working for the *Swansea Evening Post* he witnessed the less privileged side of life and it was at this time that he began to move towards socialism.

In 1936 he joined the Auxiliary Air Force, certain that armed conflict was going to break out in Europe very soon. He qualified as a pilot and joined No 601 (County of London) Squadron. In 1939 he found himself flying night-time fighter patrols over the Channel, a task with which he became more and more frustrated, and he arranged to do something about it. As a result, in April 1940 he was sent to Turkey with the nominal title of Assistant Air Attaché. In fact he was a member of the Balkan Intelligence Service. In this capacity he worked in the former Yugoslavia and in Bulgaria until the Germans invaded. He had to be smuggled out of Sofia in March 1941.

He then joined 73 (F) Squadron in Egypt, and was shot down on 7 July 1941 as he was attempting to give support to the barges supplying the besieged fortress of Tobruk. He crash-landed in a company of enemy soldiers and was sent to Germany. Reading a German newspaper on the train he saw a photograph of himself, and read with astonishment that he was apparently an explosives expert and a dangerous member of the British Secret Service.

At Oflag XXIB in Schubin Crawley was one of the escapers who left the camp through the tunnel in the camp cesspool. He was recaptured at Innsbruck. His papers passed muster, but he gave himself away through sheer exhaustion, and was returned to Schubin only briefly before being moved to Stalag Luft III. There he became information officer and camp interpreter. It was his unpleasant duty to report the news that fifty of the 'Great Escape' officers had been shot.

Crawley attempted several more escapes but was always recaptured. In Stalag Luft III he began to collect the materials that would later become *Escape from Germany*, an account of the various escape attempts he had witnessed. The notes for the book survived the forced marches at the end of the war, and the first version of the book appeared in 1956. The full text did not become available until 1985, for security reasons, when it was published by HMSO.

Crawley wasted no time after his release in May 1945. In the General Election the same year he won a seat at Buckingham for Labour, for which he had been adopted before the war, and he became Parliamentary Under-Secretary of State for Air in 1950. He lost his seat in a closely fought election in 1951 and went back to making documentary films. In 1962 he was back in Parliament, this time representing West Derbyshire as a Conservative, and his former Labour colleagues took a dim view of his change of heart. Moreover, the Conservative party seemed unwilling to pay heed to his warnings about communist influence in the unions, and when he was asked to choose between television and politics in 1967 he chose television.

Aidan Crawley died in 1993, aged 85.

PETER FANSHAWE

Peter Fanshawe was one of the principal organizers of the 'Great Escape' from Stalag Luft III in March 1944. Of the three tunnels that were started from North compound (Tom, Dick, and Harry) only Harry was completed. Seventy-six PoWs broke out. Three made it back to England, twenty-three were returned to captivity and fifty were machine-gunned by the Gestapo on Hitler's orders.

Fanshawe was due to be one of the first out of the tunnel, since he was one of the chief organizers, but he was transferred out of the camp a few days before the escape. This piece of hard luck might well have saved his life.

Throughout his captivity he was a tireless and creative nurturer of escape plans, and he is credited as being the one who invented the 'trouser bag' method of disposing of sand from the tunnels. Sand and earth from the tunnels had to be disposed of in such a way as not to bring attention to the fact that a tunnel was in progress and, as the sand was often of a different colour than the surface sand, this required some care. Fanshawe suggested that the men make long, thin bags for sand, to be placed inside their trousers and held shut with a string. They could then walk around the camp, releasing small amounts of sand and shuffling their feet as a way to make it blend in. If they encountered a guard they just kept walking normally, pulling the drawstring closed. This seemingly simple idea was a huge success in dealing with a difficult problem. Arthur Durand, in *Stalag Luft III: The Secret Story* (1988) claims that it took eighteen thousand individual trips by the men who carried these bags, who earned the name 'Penguins', to disperse the spare dirt, and that an additional sixty-eight tons of sand were hidden beneath the floor of the theatre for this one escape.

Fanshawe had been the observer on a Blackburn Skua dive bomber when he was shot down over Trondheim. The Skuas were part of 803 Naval Air Squadron operating from the aircraft carrier *Ark Royal*, and they had been sent to bomb the battleships *Scharnhorst* and *Gneisenau*, on 13 June 1940. Five days earlier these two ships had sunk the aircraft carrier *Glorious* and her two escorts off northern Norway. Fanshawe's flight was intended to exact revenge, but the whole plan was badly flawed from the start. The battleships were heavily defended by fighters and anti-aircraft vessels, there was no cloud cover, and that far north in

June there was almost no darkness to provide any element of surprise. The attack soon ran into trouble. Fanshawe's bomb missed. In fact only one bomb was seen to land on the *Scharnhorst* that day, a 500lb bomb, which rolled off the armour and into the sea without exploding. This proves the point, made later in the war, that a 500lb bomb dropped from that height could not have penetrated the deck armour, and that raids like these were futile. Of fifteen attacking Skuas, eight were shot down.

Fanshawe's plane, piloted by Lieutenant Commander Casson, the unit's Commanding Officer, was pursued by an Me109 and, after evasive action during which Fanshawe took a bullet to the shoulder and the fuel tank was ruptured, Casson put the plane down in a fjord. They were picked up by a Norwegian in a rowing boat.

Fanshawe was awarded the OBE in 1946. After the war he commanded the sloop *Amethyst* in the Korean war, and was mentioned in dispatches, winning the DSC. Following this he was loaned to the Royal Australian Navy at HMAS *Albatross*, a naval air station, from 1954 to 1957. In 1962 he became the vice-president of the Admiralty Interview Board and was Naval Assistant to the Naval Secretary from 1964 to 1966, when he retired with a CBE.

Captain Peter Fanshawe was born on Sept. 13, 1911, educated at Dartmouth Royal Naval College, and died in Feb. 1994, aged 82.

RICHARD KELLETT

Born on 24 October 1905, Richard Kellett was educated at Bedford School and decided on a career in the RAF. The story is that he had wanted to join the Navy until one day he heard that RAF cadets at Cranwell were given a motorcycle as standard issue. He promptly switched to the RAF.

In the 1920s he served in Iraq, where, on one occasion, he force-landed in the desert. He was rescued in the nick of time by another pilot, whose aircraft was chased by hostile tribesmen as it took off. In 1936 he became an adviser on engineering for the Imperial Japanese Air Force, and had the unusual distinction of receiving from the Emperor the Order of the Sacred Treasure of Japan in appreciation of his services.

In 1937 he was back in England commanding 148 Squadron, which was equipped with Vickers Wellesley bombers. On November 5 to 7 the following year, as leader of the RAF Long Range Development Unit, he piloted one of the two Wellesleys that flew non-stop from Ismailia in Egypt to Australia – a distance of 7,159 miles in just over 48 hours. This feat hit the world headlines and he received the AFC in 1939, and the Royal Aero Club's Britannia Trophy, in recognition of the achievement.

The Wellesley was the precursor of the Wellington bomber, and it had the same geodetic construction, pioneered by Sir Barnes Wallis, which made that aircraft so rugged. It is arguable that Kellett's long-distance achievement significantly helped in bringing attention to the value of this type of aircraft, which was to prove to be the mainstay of Britain's bomber force in the early days of the war.

A year after his long distance flight he became the commander of 149 Squadron, flying Wellingtons, and he led them in a series of daylight raids against German warships in December 1939. This took him over Wilhelmshaven and Kiel and over the Heligoland Bight, which was heavily defended by German anti-aircraft installations and patrolled by fighters. Kellett led formations of as many as twenty-four aircraft, from several Squadrons based in East Anglia, into this area, known as 'the hornet's nest' because of the ferocious opposition. On one occasion a flight of twenty-two Wellingtons was so badly mauled that it was reduced to just ten, three of which were so badly shot up that they crash landed on their return. The fights weren't always so one-sided, however, and one raid claimed a total of twelve Me109 and Me110 fighters shot down. In 1940 Kellett was awarded the DFC.

Kellett was captured when he decided to take part in a raid on Tobruk, in North Africa, in 1942. Since he was officially an administrator at the time, this was an unlucky turn of events. He arrived in Stalag Luft III and, as a Group Captain, he became the Senior British Officer. He was SBO at the time of the Wooden Horse escape, and his powers of leadership were part of what made that escape possible, since he was the person who decided whether or not a plan was viable and which ones should be allowed to proceed. His leadership was important in other ways as well. As the senior representative in the camp it was his task to negotiate with the Germans about camp conditions. He was responsible for the lives of all the Allied airmen in the camp, and the skilful handling of the day-to-day conflicts could make a huge difference to the overall conditions. There is no doubt that his leadership helped to save many lives.

While a PoW he received a parcel one day that contained a single golf club. Delighted, he improvised a ball and then set about creating an eighteen-hole course, using tree stumps as holes. This, he always said, was one of the highlights of his time as a PoW. It was to give rise to some misunderstandings later when families back in England received letters that mentioned the camp's 'golf course' and began to wonder just what exactly was going on.

After the war Kellett was placed in charge of training in the Middle East, but in 1946 he left the RAF on health grounds, retiring with the rank of Air Commodore. He then worked in Rhodesia, in South Africa, and returned to Britain in 1965. He then bought a boat, intending to spend his retirement sailing the Mediterranean. Upon arriving in Majorca, however, he and his wife decided they need sail no further. He died in 1990, aged 84.

OLIVER PHILPOT

Oliver Lawrence Spurling Philpot was born in Vancouver, British Columbia, on 6 March 1913. He was educated in England at Radley and at Worcester College, Oxford, where he first learned to fly with the University Air Squadron.

After university he joined Unilever in 1934 as a trainee

manager. Two years later he was appointed assistant commercial secretary of its Home Margarine Executive.

In August 1939 he reported for full-time RAF service, was commissioned as a pilot officer and posted to 42 Squadron, Coastal Command. At the time they were flying obsolete Vickers Vildebeeste torpedo bombers, but by June 1940 they had been re-equipped with Bristol Beauforts. He saw action in the Norwegian campaign – on one occasion pressing ahead with an attack on Christiansand despite having sustained heavy damage to the aircraft. Returning with a crew that were either dead or dying, he managed to reach Leuchars in Scotland, where he made a successful wheels-up landing.

He was shot down on 11 December 1941 by a German escort vessel as he was attempting to attack a large merchant ship in the middle of a convoy in the North Sea. He managed to ditch the Beaufort successfully, giving the crew time to escape before the aircraft broke in two and sank. They then spent two nights in their dinghy before being picked up by an enemy vessel. Their first days in captivity were spent recovering from the effects of exposure.

In 1943 he joined the escape plans of Flight Lieutenant Eric Williams and Lieutenant Michael Codner, R.A., who had contrived the idea of digging an escape tunnel underneath a wooden exercise horse, over which other prisoners were encouraged to vault. The operation was unusual in that it involved placing the horse precisely over the disguised tunnel entrance in the middle of the sports ground each day. This allowed the tunneler concealed in the horse to descend into the hole and dig towards the wire. This came to be known as the Wooden Horse, because, like the Greeks at Troy, a wooden structure was used to disguise what was going on – in this case a movement inside the wire heading outwards. The Germans did not suspect that a tunnel could be built in this unusual fashion, especially as the wire was more than 100 feet away, and they soon became accustomed to the vaulting horse.

On 29 October 1943 at 1pm two men were carried out to the tunnel. Codner entered the tunnel and remained in it. Williams sealed him in and returned in the horse. The afternoon count was managed so that Codner was not missed. Then at 5pm Williams and Philpot were carried out and sealed themselves in. They waited until dark, completed the last section of the tunnel, and, pushing the loose sand behind them, broke out. Their tunnel emerged barely a foot from where they had predicted.

Philpot was fortunate in that he had worked in Germany before the war and could speak and understand German quite well. He posed as a Norwegian margarine salesman, carried a small case and stuck a pipe in his mouth to disguise his accent. He had also grown a moustache which he had trimmed at the last moment to a suitably Hitler-like dimension. He looked, he thought, like a quisling ought to. Codner and Williams were disguised as workmen.

The advantages of pretending to be Norwegian were not just to do with accent, however. Real German papers were hard to come by and hard to forge successfully, because everyone in the outside world knew what they should look like. By choosing a Norwegian identity it would be more likely that any mistakes in the documents would go undetected. It also allowed for some creative guesswork by the forgers. The aim was to try to make the paperwork look convincing rather than worrying about an absolute accuracy they could not hope to achieve. After all, none of them had any idea what the originals looked like. And, since foreign documents all had to be approved by Nazi officialdom, a series of authentic-looking Third Reich stamps would lend immediate credibility to any document – and there were plenty of examples of those because every piece of mail that entered the camp was examined, stamped and re-stamped. The Norwegian identity could also be useful if anyone looked askance at what Philpot was wearing. Odd clothing could be explained away as foreign custom. And in his black Homburg, his RAF greatcoat and Fleet Air Arm trousers he must have looked a little unusual.

He walked to Sagan station and bought a ticket to Frankfurt-on-Oder, studiously ignoring his fellow escapees on the platform. The following morning he bought a ticket on the local slow train to Kustrin, then caught the Königsberg express. This was so crowded that he went to sleep sitting on his suitcase, and when the train lurched he fell off, uttering a loud 'Damn!' as he did so. The other passengers just laughed.

While on the train his papers were examined by a plain-clothes policeman, and despite some anxious moments (the identity photograph had not been stamped with the official seal) he was allowed to continue. The forgeries had held up. He took another train at Dirschau, then the fast train to Danzig.

In Danzig, which he reached less than 24 hours after emerging from the tunnel, he treated himself to a glass of beer in the station refreshment hall, which was full of German soldiers. He then took a room in a hotel, only to discover that he had to share it with another person. He pretended to be heavily asleep when the other man came in, and slipped out early to avoid any possibility of conversation.

At Danzig docks he took a ferry ride around the harbour, noting the layout of the docks and some promising-looking ships to stow away on. In the evening he returned, ducked under the wire and hauled himself up the mooring cables of the chosen vessel. He hid in the coal bunkers. The next morning, after the ship had got well clear of the harbour, he made his presence known. In this he was a little premature. The Captain told him he had to get off. Another crew member hid him in the bilges, presumably until all chance of German surprise inspections had passed, and he emerged several hours later to a far pleasanter reception from the same Captain. At the British Legation in Stockholm he met up with Codner and Williams, to much hilarity, and they eventually were flown home.

Stolen Journey, published in 1950, is the full account of his exploits, and is one of the best pieces of writing on this now legendary episode. The same year the film *The Wooden Horse*, based on his book, was released.

After his return Philpot did not fly any more missions and in 1944 he was appointed as senior scientific officer at the Air Ministry. He was demobilized in 1946 and returned to civilian life, where he had a very successful career in business, working for Unilever, Walls & Son, eventually becoming managing director of Fropax Eskimo Food, which later became Findus. In 1978 he retired after having been for four years the managing director of Remploy.

His other activities were equally energetic. He was chairman of the RAF Escaping Society; he served on the National Advisory Council on Employment for Disabled People, as well as being an administrator for Help the Aged. He also found time to be a manager at the St. Bride Foundation Institute. In addition he gave occasional talks and lectures about his escape. When Philpot spoke he always mentioned his gratitude to 'Red' Hunter, who had forged his papers. He met Jim at one such talk in Esher, Surrey, and they enjoyed catching up on old times.

Philpot's courage and ingenuity have, perhaps, tended to overshadow one main fact about this escape; simply put, it is that this was one of the very few times when all the escapers made it back to England. It is worth remembering that of all the escape attempts from Stalag Luft III very few were successful. The Great Escape of seventy-six men through the tunnel 'Harry' produced only three 'home runs'. Everyone else was re-captured and, on Hitler's orders, fifty were shot. This brought the grand total of escapers who reached home from this camp to just six.

Oliver Philpot was awarded the DFC in 1941, and the MC in 1944. He died in May 1993, aged 80.

Appendix 2

Prison Camp Life

For many people, when reading the words Stalag Luft III, there is a tendency to lump all that one knows together and to assume that it was just one large camp. In fact, this is not helpful. There were several camps clustered together which had this name, all adjacent to each other, but not accessible. Jim was in East compound, which stood next to Centre compound. These two were the oldest parts of the camp. Centre compound was originally intended for the NCOs.

North compound was constructed in early 1943, and British and Americans were moved into it that March. Many hardened escapers were placed in North compound, and it was from there that the 'Great Escape' was launched. Before this could happen, however, the Americans were removed and placed in South compound, in September, while Centre compound was emptied of NCOs and more Americans were placed there, together with some British. West compound opened in winter 1943, and in spring 1944 Belaria compound was opened. Neither of these two achieved much in the way of escapes, and when the 'Great Escape' ended in tragedy in March 1944 there was a further disincentive for the occupants of these new camps to get to work at escaping. The prisoners were told on 6 April 1944, that fifty of the escapers had been shot, and they saw that the situation had changed.

It is apparent that the experiences in each compound were not identical, and when the prisoners were marched out in 1945, the American contingent was marched in a completely different direction, to Stalag VIIA, near Moosburg, to be liberated by General Patton.

3

The Tunnel at Oflag XXIB, Schubin

This tunnel has been described in some detail by Lord Barber, who was Chancellor of the Exchequer from 1970 to 1974, and his account has been reprinted in *The RAF at War* (Ian Allan Books), as well as in *The Sunday Express*, 12 February 1984.

The tunnel at Schubin was constructed by removing parts of a brick wall that made up one side of the main latrine pit. The latrine itself was a huge fifty-seat structure. The challenge was to construct a trap door in this wall without falling into the pit itself. Several seats were hinged to allow the escapers easy access, and, as Jim Hunter recalled, "We all knew which seats not to use." Behind the trap, under the concrete floor, a large chamber approximately six feet high, ten feet wide, and twelve feet long was excavated. This was, by tunneling standards at the time, an enormous space. It proved extremely useful as an area in which to store earth from the tunnel, some of which was then disposed of in the latrine pit. The Polish workmen who came to the camp periodically to pump out the pit must have noticed what was going on, but they said nothing, and, more to the point, they were careful never to pump out the pit entirely, so there was always some sewage under which to hide the sand from the digging.

This tunnel was on a scale never before attempted in any other camp. It ran for 300 feet to a potato clamp beyond the wire and was dug to a depth of 20 feet to avoid all underground obstacles. It had a fully supported roof, as well as pumped air provided by a man working a large bellows made from a kitbag, and was lit by fat lamps. Even so it was cramped; it was only two feet high and two feet wide. In addition the air that the tunnelers needed at the work face could only come from one place, the latrine, so it was hardly ideal. On the night of 3 March 1943, forty men (Barber claims only thirty) made their way beyond the wire, using the potato clamp as cover from which they could run to the woods after the searchlights had gone past.

The following morning *Appell* was chaotic. At first the prisoners lined up in groups of four, rather than groups of five. This brought the numbers out at too many. They were then made to stand in fives, as usual. When the count was complete the Commandant was faced with forty prisoners unaccounted for. He decided that such a large number could not possibly have escaped and so the Germans searched the camp, looking for the hidden men. This took several hours, giving the escapees a better chance to get clear. By now the Commandant was fearful of telling his superiors that forty men were unaccounted for, and so another search was begun.

Eventually all the escapees were caught, except for two who, according to Barber, were shot while making a run for it. A more accurate account, based on the retrieval of one body from the coast of Denmark, suggests that these two were rowing towards neutral Sweden when their boat was run down by a larger ship in the fog.

The failure to achieve any home runs on this occasion may seem like a poor overall performance, but it is worth remembering that the escape caused a huge amount of extra effort for the Germans. Troops who might otherwise have been at the front lines were forced to man checkpoints, conduct searches through woods and open spaces, and generally waste valuable resources. From the point of view of German morale, it helped to make ordinary travel more onerous because of increased random searches, and this in turn added a sense that events were not under control in the Reich. Arthur Durand's book, *Stalag Luft III, The Secret Story*, (William Kimber, 1988) makes this quite plain: "The escape diverted more than four thousand German troops to the area and, for a period of a week or more, held the full attention of at least one thousand policemen and home guardsmen."

Each person travelling through the Reich was expected to have several of a number of documents ready for inspection. It is tempting for us to underestimate how difficult the forger's task was, but even a quick glance at the number of pieces of paper that each person was expected to possess will change that perception. Here is a general list of what was required.

1. The *Dienstausweise*: a brown card that entitled the bearer to be on Wehrmacht property;

2. The *Urlaubsscheine*: a yellow card that showed the bearer was permitted to take leave from the workplace. This was usually issued to foreign workers;

3. The *Ruckkehrscheine*: a pink form that showed a foreign worker was being sent back to his country;

4. The *Kennkarte*: the standard light grey identity card;

5. The *Carte d'Identité*: the French identity card;

6. The *Sichtvermerk*: a visa;

7. The *Ausweise und Vorlaufige Ausweise*: passes and temporary passes;

8. The *Polizeitliche Bescheinigung*: a police pass that allowed a foreign worker to be in certain areas;

9. Various letters supplied by employers, on headed notepaper, which explained what the individual was supposed to be doing. To this could be added business cards and so on.

Not everyone needed all of these, but the reader can deduce the range of documentation required for each escaper. Oliver Philpot would not have needed a *Dienstausweise*, nor the French *Carte d'Identité*, but he would have had everything else, including a letter that said his Norwegian passport was being held by the German police.

Appendix 4

The Casualty Rate

Jim refers briefly to the 'chop rate', or the rate at which aircrew were killed. This is a difficult statistic to quantify, since aircraft were lost not only to enemy action but also to accidents, mechanical failure and navigational errors. A crew that did not return could have fallen victim to a number of circumstances, and there was no way to tell which factor, or combination, was to blame.

Jim tells us that Tommy Kerr and Pilot Officers Graham and Stockley, his friends at the Waterbeach, were killed. He also mentions Jock Maclean, who was killed after Jim was shot down. In fact he doesn't mention anyone he knew as having survived, outside his own crew. Roy Nesbit's book makes the point that during the time he was with 217 Squadron (which overlapped the time Jim was there) twenty-four aircraft were lost, and since the usual complement of crews on a squadron was only ten, that meant a huge turnover of men. He states that he only knew of one crew that got out of a ditched Beaufort and survived. He does not give the names but it is possible he is referring to Jim's crew. He mentions one other crew that got out after ditching, but all died of hypothermia before they were picked up. He estimates that Bomber Command lost 30% of aircraft over thirty sorties (*Woe to The Unwary*, p.156).

Statitics supplied from the Imperial War Museum indicate that during the war a crew could expect to survive an average of ten missions before being shot down. Of the 125,000 men flying in Bomber Command 55,500 were killed by the war's end, and

18,000 were wounded or became PoWs, according to W. R. Chorley's *Royal Air Force Bomber Command Losses of the Second World War*. 8,600 bombers of all types were lost overall. Historian W. G. Sebald, writing in *A Natural History of Destruction* (forthcoming), states that Allied aircrew in World War Two suffered a 60% death rate (excerpted in the *New Yorker* Nov. 2, 2002).

These figures on their own are misleading, because not all phases of the war were the same. For example, in the air campaigns of 1940 the loss rate of British aircraft was shocking. The Fairey Battles sent to attack the pontoon bridges at Sedan in France were slaughtered. Of seventy-one bombers sent out only thirty-one returned (this is according to the home page of RAF Waddington, which can be regarded as authoritative). This rate of loss was not unusual during the battle for France. Blenheims and Battles were destroyed in huge numbers, often on the ground. Clearly this was the time of the war when losses were most disastrous and the statistics are therefore unrepresentative.

Beauforts, likewise, were thrown into battle with the clear sense that they were expendable. The planned raids against the *Bismarck*, mentioned by Jim, indicate this, for the crews knew they would not have sufficient fuel to return. Later in the war, in January 1942, a very similar strategy was proposed for bombing the *Tirpitz* in Trondheim fjord. Beaufort crews were briefed to attack the battleship, then to head for Sweden and bail out before their planes ran out of fuel and fell out of the sky. Bad weather prevented that plan from reaching fruition. Yet the message was clear: aircraft and crews were expendable.

Another factor in the casualty rate was surely the British belief in not putting a lot of heavy armour plate in their aircraft, at least in the early part of the war. In a Beaufort the extra weight would have been a handicap in an otherwise underpowered plane. In the Wellington the rear gunner could certainly have used something more substantial than the tiny square of steel between the barrels of his guns, especially as the death of the rear gunner usually meant the aircraft was helpless to attack from the rear.

Why was this situation not remedied? A clue may lie in the order issued by the head of Bomber Command, Sir Arthur Harris, that all armour plate be removed from the crew cockpits of Lancasters so that they could carry a greater weight of bombs. By contrast the B-17 Flying Fortress had far more in the way of defensive armament and armour plate. Unfortunately it carried a lesser bombload as a result. But it was much better placed when it sustained damage from daylight fighters, and many tales are told of Fortresses limping home after taking heavy damage. Perhaps it was felt that the armour plate was more necessary in daylight bombers.

Of the airmen who were shot down only one in five managed to bail out. This statistic was probably due to the British habit of having crew place their parachutes in racks that were often some distance from where they were working. Aircraft were simply not designed so that the crews could get out quickly if the plane itself was damaged. Those vital few seconds needed to locate one's parachute and clip it on, before finding an escape hatch in a tumbling aircraft, were just not available. Jim's parachute was a clip-on item. For him the point was academic most of the time, since the Beaufort routinely operated at heights which were well below the recommended altitude for using parachutes. Even so, parachutes could work from exceptionally low levels. Jim's PoW friend Roger Simmons, who was shot down flying a Spitfire, bailed out at an estimated 150 feet or less, and lived to tell the tale. Fighter pilots had an advantage because they were harnessed to their parachutes, and the pack doubled as a seat. Simmons survived the initial attack, incidentally, largely because of the armour plate behind his seat which withstood most of the cannon and machine-gun fire.

Bibliography

There have been many books written about PoW life and I offer here a selection for the reader. Those who wish to undertake detailed historical study of individual camps would do well to consult the bibliographies in the back of particular studies. For example, Arthur Durand's admirable study *Stalag Luft III: The Secret Story* (1988) lists much manuscript material from Wright-Patterson Air Force base, Ohio; from the American Red Cross Headquarters, Washington; from The National Archives; personal correspondence, and so on. Much of this material remains unpublished and is not accessible to the general reader. At this time most of it is not available on the world wide web, either. I have not repeated those references here. I have listed only printed books which can be found in libraries, and which might interest the enquiring reader.

Buckham, Robert, *Forced March to Freedom: An Illustrated Diary of Two Forced Marches and the Interval between, January to May 1945*, Ontario, 1984.

Brickhill, Paul, *The Great Escape*, Greenwich, Conn., 1950.

Carlson, Lewis H. *We Were Each Other's Prisoners*, New York, 1998.

Crawley, Aidan, *Escape from Germany: A History of RAF Escapes During the War*, New York, 1956. Reprinted with additions, HMSO, 1984.

Daniel, Eugene L. Jr. *In the Presence of Mine Enemies: Memoirs of German Prisoner of War Life, February 16 1943 to April 29, 1945*. Attleboro, Mass, 1985.

James, B. A., *Moonless Night: One Man's Struggle for Freedom, 1940-1945*, London, 1983.

Morgan, Guy, *P.O.W*, New York, 1946.

Neary, Bob, *Stalag Luft III: Sagan . . . Nurenberg . . . Moosberg. A Collection of German Prison Camp Sketches with Descriptive Text Based on Personal Experiences*, North Wales, Pa., 1946.

Philpot, Oliver, *Stolen Journey*, London, 1950.

Williams, Eric, *The Wooden Horse*, New York, 1949.

Sources of further information on Beauforts and 217 Squadron.

Barker, Ralph, *The Ship Busters*, London, 1957.

Gibbs, R.P.M, *Not Peace But a Sword*, London, 1943.

Gibbs, R.P.M, *Torpedo Leader on Malta*, London, 1989.

Nesbit, Roy Conyers, *Woe To The Unwary: A Memoir of Low-Level Bombing Operations in 1941*. London, 1981.

Nesbit, Roy Conyers, *Torpedo Airmen: Missions with Bristol Beauforts 1940-42*, London, 1983.

Operations Record Book, 217 Squadron, Public Record Office, Kew.

Robertson, Bruce, *Beaufort Special*, Shepperton, Surrey, 1976.

War Diary of Scharnhorst, Ministry of Defence, Naval Historical Branch.

Index

Prison camps had their own coding system.

Oflag was short for Offizierlager – for officers only.

Stalag stood for Stammlager, a camp for other ranks.

Stalag Luft was a contraction of Stammlager Luftwaffe, where the addition of the word Luft indicated a camp for airmen only.

Dulag was short for Durchgangslager – a transit camp.

Marlag was a contraction of Marinelager – a camp for navy prisoners.

The numerals that appear after the names of each camp do not indicate how many of such camps there were. They refer only to the administrative area in which each was situated.